9/02

D0867511

EDIZIONI

Thompson, Ventulett, Stainback & Associates

Inside/Outside:
The Architecture of TVS

Thomas D. Galloway   Sara Hart

Edizioni Press

First published in the
United States of America
by Edizioni Press, Inc.
469 West 21st Street
New York, New York 10011
Mail@edizionipress.com

ISBN: 0-9662230-8-X

Library of Congress Catalogue
Card Number: 00 - 106755

Printed in Italy

Design:
bianca graphic design

Editorial Director:
Anthony Iannacci
Assistant Editor:
Jamie Schwartz
Associate Editor:
Kara Janeczko
Editorial Assistant:
Aaron Seward

Front Cover:
Salt Palace Convention Center,
Salt Lake City, Utah

Culture, Organization, and Design Priorities

Thomas D. Galloway

What distinguishes Thompson, Ventulett, Stainback and Associates from other design organizations? From the professional and popular media, we know TVS's regional, national, and increasingly international reputation. We know that the firm has been consistently ranked among *Building Design and Construction's* "Top Design Firms" over the past 17 years and is continuously ranked among the top firms in *Engineering News Record's* annual listing of the largest firms in the nation. In the following pages, we can observe a good deal of this large architectural firm's work, but we will also come to realize that, in the conventional sense of signature architecture, there is no "TVS style."

The firm's deliberate focus on certain project types is fundamental to its diversity. TVS has worked on corporate and commercial office centers, retail centers, convention centers, hotels, resorts and conference centers, entertainment and hospitality venues, educational and cultural arts facilities, and performance halls. What is not very well known, however, except perhaps by its clients, is the distinct ways in which this firm goes about making these many different types of buildings. It is the synergism of its characteristics and processes that makes TVS special. In experiencing any one of its projects, the viewer senses the positive, active interdependence of the firm's uncommon traits.

Promenade Two, Atlanta, GA (1990). The tower offers a stark contrast to the more traditional surrounding architecture, signaling a new urban architectural vocabulary for the city of Atlanta.

The combination of the firm's studio organization and varied project types has a powerful impact on the firm's social organization. TVS is effectively the equivalent of ten mid-sized architectural firms. Each studio is allowed important degrees of freedom for creative expression, entrepreneurship, openness, and design autonomy, qualities important to the development and retention of its design staff. J. Thomas Porter, Large Scale Retail Planning and Design, said, "As a studio organized firm, TVS maintains its freshness which is reinforced by continued development of new, young design talent."

Ray C. Hoover, III, Mixed-Use Development, senses this in another way. "TVS is a great place to learn architecture. You are allowed to go where the opportunity is; you can work where you are interested, relative to design and building type." Thus, it is not surprising that TVS views its people as its most important asset. The firm is able to retain its intellectual and design capital over time, thereby maintaining design continuity.

It is also important to note that, since the firm's inception, the founding partners have taken lead responsibilities in the business of architecture, the design of architecture, and the personnel of architecture. The firm still uses these important dimensions to define and measure the success of their designs. TVS is always conscious of the design of the project itself, the project's profitability, its technology, the client's satisfaction, and the rigor devoted to each of these dimensions. Formal design reviews, much like those studio critiques or juries in architectural schools, the juries in this case made up of senior designers from other TVS studios or retained for specialized areas of expertise, are scheduled throughout the design and development of each project.

Founding Principal Thomas W. Ventulett, III noted, "The passion of the firm remains with design... Architecture is the design of space – both interior and exterior – not just the buildings themselves." The bottom line, according to Ventulett, is that people are affected by the spaces they inhabit. The formal design review process lifts the project to a higher level and captures the diverse expertise of the firm within each project.

In this examination, we might also identify two important common threads that weave through the various design studios of TVS. They both focus, not on style, but on design philosophy: 1) the "design reach," a phrase used to imply a continually raised expectation of design excellence and innovation in each TVS project, and 2) a particular focus on the quality of public space in

Equifax Headquarters, Atlanta, GA (2000). The design for the Equifax corporate office building conveys the corporation's innovative high-tech culture with its sleek, contemporary exterior. Situated on a prime triangular site in midtown Atlanta, the building shape is equally intriguing to the public from all directions.

Three First Union, Charlotte, NC (2000). The high quality materials and finishes found on the exterior of the tower are carried into the interior public lobbies. The polished marble and granite floor and wainscot and the Venetian plaster walls are highlighted with inset stainless steel accents and custom designed light fixtures.

all the studios' projects. Ventulett said, "It is the culture of the firm to reach for a new level of understanding and the development of a new design characteristic that adds quality, value and client/customer satisfaction. Each project is a search for something different, without rejecting out-of-hand tradition."

When speaking of corporate facilities and convention centers, Michael H. Ezell, Public Assembly Facilities, expressed the joy of finding the "unexpected" building element in each project, and creating something larger than the project itself. One example is the public space and streetscape created at 14th /15th and Peachtree Streets in Midtown Atlanta by its various buildings, including Promenade Two.

For retail/shopping centers, Porter felt it was of utmost importance to elevate the design of retail space to a new level. This is seen, according to Porter, not only in the redesign of existing shopping centers like Phipps Plaza in Atlanta, but in the firm's "big box" projects such as the large brownfield Atlantic Steel project.

For Andy McLean, Convention Centers, "These projects [with long cycle times] never get stale, all are in different cities with differing contexts. I always ask how a particular element of each project can be made better: where and how far can I reach?"

The scale and importance of these large-scale projects' urban sites deepen these sentiments and philosophies. The lead designers are impassioned, according to Ezell, "...with the realization of the awesome responsibility of creating the built environment, made even more ominous given the size and magnitude of the projects that TVS designs, from convention centers and high-rise office buildings to mega-scale shopping complexes." Noted often as "soul-less" places, the sites of many of the firm's convention centers have been located on abandoned railroad yards, on top of rights-of-way- places that must be transformed from places of abandonment to places of destination.

In these types of projects especially, TVS remains very committed to certain design criteria. The space must look and feel appropriate – as if it has always been there; each project must have a human scale, even monumental buildings; each project must provide simplicity of way-finding and pleasantness in moving through the space; the space must provide for activities/opportunities within and without.

Perhaps these qualities are best seen in TVS's approach to interior design, a key element of the firm. Steven W. Clem,

Three First Union, Charlotte, NC (2000). The sleek granite and glass tower, accented with stainless steel ribs, culminates with a creative and dynamic glass art sculpture designed by Kenneth vonRoenn. The light reflected from the glass spires changes color according to the viewer's vantage point.

Interior Design, suggests that the key lies in the proportional relationships. In large-scale projects with monumental spaces, the human body is the point of reference. In more intimate settings, it is not the human body, but the human hand and eye that are the units of reference because tactile senses, lighting, and color provide a sense of comfort in these spaces. He suggests: "Users and clients sense the difference made by design (good or bad), although they may not be able to express exactly what they like or dislike about the space in specific terms. Interiors are special. Users can relate to them differently from buildings. Their homes, their clothes, the restaurants and other places they inhabit are specific points of reference and comparison. Everything is in the detail."

The firm's design innovations go beyond TVS and affect the design profession as a whole. This is most dramatic in two particular areas: the design of retail space and the design of convention centers. TVS has moved retail design in an entirely new direction, using the metaphor of the room in the case of Phipps Plaza, or the metaphor of villages in its current work on the Atlantic Steel Project. But it is even more apparent in convention center design. Here, TVS has changed the way the design profession regards these facilities, as well as the way it approaches them. TVS was the first to move away from the clear span structures of convention center design. The firm recognized that owners were investing large sums of money into a structure type that was not necessary to the achievement of their goals. Consequently, TVS introduced the concept of corridors, concourses, and "rooms" that brought a totally new organization of space to the design of these facilities. TVS's design approach set a new standard for the industry, in much the same way as John Portman set a new standard for hotel design with the atrium. It is not coincidental that the scale and urban-forming qualities of these two different project types have had equally significant impacts on the central cities in which they are located.

So we can see the firm's mechanisms for transferring design memory and experience to each new project, but what of the future? Changes in technology, as well as changes in consumer, tenant, and owner demands, are catalyzing a need for design and development of new additions to the built environment. It is axiomatic to say that today's design firms are challenged as never before to understand fully the industries behind the building types, whether it is retailing, tourism, hospitality, corporate business or others.

Atlantic Station, Atlanta, GA (2000). The master plan for the reuse of the former Atlantic Steel site will create an environment that supports residential, business, and entertainment uses on a restored brownfield site in the center of the city of Atlanta. The mixed-use village setting will encourage an in-town living environment.

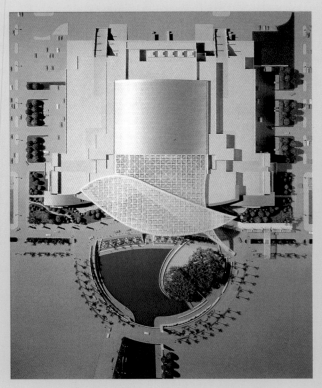

Puerto Rico Convention and Trade Center, San Juan, Puerto Rico (2004). The Puerto Rico Convention Center is the centerpiece of a new mixed-use district for the city of San Juan. At the culmination of a canal, the entrance plaza, with its dynamic waveform roof structure, focuses on the water feature and the district beyond. The indoor/outdoor space is envisioned as a community-gathering place for conventions and local civic events.

This is an issue becoming much more important than it has ever been in the past. Porter observed that in the early 1970s, retail design resembled a "cookie cutter" process with an easily replicated template. But this project type had two special qualities. First, it was not on the "radar screen" for quality design; and secondly, as a building type, it touched more people than any other. Similarly, Andy McLean, Convention Centers, noted that convention center design in this same time period was grim and very introspective. "As a project type, it was not appreciated as a design-centered element of the built environment."

All of this has changed: higher levels of design emphasis; increased understanding and appreciation of the value-added "bottom-line;" importance of design excellence to owners and tenants; increasing expectations of the end users, and hence competition for employees. Coupled with these are equally rapid changes in technology, which include the increasing importance of "smart buildings" that make the design, construction, and maintenance increasingly efficient, but more complex.

Given the pace of change and the anticipatory quality of their designs, one might assert that TVS is already designing for the future. The partners expect the dimensions I've touched upon to hold continued importance. In addition, their work reflects an ever-growing concern for the health and well-being of people in the workplace and in other environments that make up the urban realm. The firm is also committed to sustainability, and to meeting the growing desire for greater flexibility in the built environment. It is clear that the nature of TVS's organization, design processes, and its people will all serve the firm well in the future.

Thomas D. Galloway, Ph.D. is Dean of the College of Architecture at Georgia Institute of Technology. He lives and works in Atlanta, Georgia.

King of Prussia, King of Prussia, PA (1994). Incorporating beautifully patterned flooring and carefully detailed stained glass skylights, the design elevated the retail mall to new heights.

Ketchum Offices, Atlanta, GA (2000). The creative culture of the Ketchum public relations firm is captured in the interior design.

Inside/Outside:
The Architecture of TVS

Sara Hart

In 1968, Macon, Georgia-based architect Bill Thompson invited two young architects, Tom Ventulett and Ray Stainback, to join him in Atlanta and form Thompson, Ventulett, Stainback & Associates. Their goal was to survive one year. They did more than survive. By 1973, they had grown to nearly 60 employees. Credit for this startling growth goes to the partners. Young, energetic, and talented, they were in the right place at the right time. Atlanta was emerging as the economic and cultural center of the New South. Its economy was growing, and businesses were building. More importantly, as is the case with most architectural firms that enjoy sustained growth, the principals were like-minded in their goals for the firm, while bringing different skills to the table. Thompson brought an astute business sense. Stainback was drawn to building technology and construction, and Ventulett was the designer. Furthermore, they understood that building types drop in and out of the market. While diversifying the practice among different industries-corporate headquarters, office towers, convention centers, sports arenas, performance halls, educational buildings, retail facilities and hotels, the three men watched their practice grow steadily and sustain itself through two severe recessions that toppled less balanced firms.

TVS's success can also be attributed to the kind of clients it has pursued. They are often civic-minded entrepreneurs and established business leaders with long-range goals and

Omni International, Atlanta, GA (1974). The successful mixed-use complex, which combines retail, office, hotel and entertainment functions under a single roof, serves as the home to CNN, the Cable News Network.

commitments to the communities where they live and do business. Often, their projects are wedded to the city's master plan for improving its urban infrastructure and stimulating economic growth. These projects are typically executed in phases over many years. When projects are successful, they outgrow their facilities and require expansions.

TVS specializes in multi-phased projects, and the firm's ability to design for the immediate project while planning for the future has brought it new commissions and, more importantly for the firm's life expectancy, repeat business. An early project, the Georgia World Congress Center, commissioned in 1974, enabled TVS to weather the crushing economic recession of the 1970s. In an era of planned obsolescence, TVS and its client chose to follow a forward-looking planning and design strategy to create a major destination for conventions, sporting events, and lodgings. The project has not only revitalized the ragged, industrial edge of downtown Atlanta but has, over nearly three decades, been successful enough to warrant three expansions, for which TVS provided master planning, programming, and architectural design. Employing its talent for maintaining architectural continuity, TVS planned and detailed each expansion that preserved the original design intentions, while addressing the needs of an evolving industry and incorporating new building technologies. The success of the Georgia World Congress Center has brought the young firm its most well-known work, the Georgia Dome, the world's largest indoor stadium, home to the Atlanta Falcons and the site of two Super Bowls and several events at the 1996 Summer Olympic Games.

As the firm grew steadily through the 1970s and '80s, its internal organization evolved into what is commonly known as the studio system. A studio is comprised of teams assigned to follow a project from inception to occupancy. This system breeds teamwork, which, in turn, ensures that TVS's design intentions are maintained from the beginning of design development through the preparation of the working drawings to construction management. The studios enjoy a certain degree of autonomy, which encourages a sense of ownership among team members who work on a particular project. It also ensures that the firm's reputation for quality control and attention to detail is maintained on every project. This structure allows experienced team leaders who run the studios to mentor young apprentices and give them the opportunity to learn all aspects of design and production. By

The Georgia Dome, Atlanta, GA (1992). Home to the Atlanta Falcons, the Georgia Dome has a uniquely designed tensile roof structure covered with translucent fiberglass-reinforced fabric.

McCormick Place Convention Center, Chicago, IL (1996). The TVS designed expansion to McCormick Place features a dramatic grand concourse, which connects all exhibit halls and function spaces to the five-acre entrance plaza.

the mid-1990s, TVS had grown to 150 employees, working in numerous studios devoted to a diverse array of building types.

While TVS's portfolio is diverse, all its projects have common challenges. They are typically large mixed-use facilities, which require the architects to reconcile multiple, complex functions under a single roof or in a collection of interdependent structures. Furthermore, especially with regard to convention centers, sporting facilities, and arts complexes, the typical TVS commission has a civic component that draws the firm into the realm of urban design. In this arena, TVS has to be considered a leader in the design of public spaces that invigorate the surrounding neighborhood. Partner Tom Ventulett considers his firm's expansion of Chicago's McCormick Place Convention Center, completed in 1996, to be one of the firm's most noteworthy urban-design achievements.

With the TVS expansion, McCormick Place Convention Center became the world's largest convention and civic center. A massive complex such as this has the potential to become an isolated and imposing compound in the city's center, but TVS successfully synthesized the mandates of several city agencies, commissions, and special interest groups into a design strategy of large-scale maneuvers. The most notable of these was the creation of a five-acre plaza with a long, crescent-shaped pool, which quickly became an animated gathering place for convention goers and area residents alike.

While TVS is lauded for its penchant for making grand exterior "urban rooms," the firm excels at interior design. As a full-service company, TVS is just as committed to applying its expertise to creating meticulously detailed interior spaces as it is to designing beautifully articulated, crisply modern buildings. In 2000, TVS Interiors, a distinct corporation within the firm, was listed in the *Atlanta Business Chronicle* as Atlanta's top interior design firm for the second year. As an integral part of the TVS team, its designers create a seamless interface between the building envelope and the interior surfaces. Rather than merely enhance the spaces, the interior designers carry the architectural intention through to the finishes. For Prince Street Technologies, a progressive supplier of custom high-end carpet in Cartersville, Georgia, TVS Interiors interpreted the company's innovative approach to design and business with sustainable, low-key finishes, reflective of the company's commitment to sustainable, environmentally responsible design.

McCormick Place Convention Center, Chicago, IL (1996). The concourse stair and escalator form a processional approach from the lobby to the upper levels.

Prince Street Technologies, Cartersville, GA (1995). The industrial aesthetic is enhanced by the unique detailing of low-maintenance, sustainable materials, which create a suitable backdrop to showcase the company's carpet products.

TVS's talent for blending architecture into the existing built environment is evident in many projects presented in this monograph. Its ability to improve the surrounding urban fabric is evident as well. Again, in 1994, the city of Philadelphia commissioned TVS to generate an economic revival with a new convention center in an area of downtown that needed redevelopment. Using granite, limestone, and brick, TVS created the Pennsylvania Convention Center, a complex that complements the architectural vocabulary of 18th century Philadelphia while giving new life to the famous Reading Train Shed by making it the main entry hall.

As of this publication, TVS is one of the largest architectural firms in the U.S. with 280 employees. New commissions, as well as expansions to former ones, are in development. The firm received a 2000 AIA National Honor Award from the American Institute of Architects for outstanding Regional and Urban Design. The award, the profession's highest recognition of excellence in design, was presented to the firm at the AIA's annual convention, which was held in the building for which TVS won the award, the Pennsylvania Convention Center. In 2001, TVS was honored again, earning the 2001 AIA National Honor Award for Architecture for McCormick Place Convention Center.

Pennsylvania Convention Center, Philadelphia, PA (1994). The carefully articulated and detailed granite, limestone, and brick façade successfully integrates the building with the urban context of Philadelphia.

Pennsylvania Convention Center, Philadelphia, PA (1994). The adaptive reuse of the Reading Train Shed for a grand entrance hall not only saved a historic landmark, but also gave the convention center a priceless asset that cannot be duplicated.

Sara Hart is a senior editor at *Architectural Record*. She holds a master's degree in architecture from Columbia University.

The World of Coca-Cola Pavilion

Atlanta, Georgia 1990

Atlanta is the headquarters of the Coca-Cola Company, and the World of Coca-Cola pavilion in Atlanta serves several purposes. It is a museum that entertains and informs visitors about one of the world's most popular products, and its landmark signage provides an iconic identity for the company in downtown Atlanta. TVS created a 47,000-square-foot building, which responds sensitively to its urban environment. The design relates to the scale and detailing of nearby architecture, which includes two churches, the Georgia State Capitol, and a historic freight depot.

The architects incorporated a globe sign, a back-lit entablature sign, and an abstracted glass bottle into the architectural imagery of the Coca-Cola pavilion. These images establish Coca-Cola as a refreshing and enduring image for the visitor. The architects designed a building with four distinctive pavilions, joined by a cross-shaped skylight atrium, which provides circulation from one pavilion to the next. Within these four pavilions, artifacts relating to the history of Coca-Cola are exhibited in more than 300 linear feet of glass and polished steel casework.

The architects conceived of each pavilion as having a distinctive exterior character. The pavilion closest to the capitol is dignified and conservative. It is sheathed in limestone, the traditional building material of the capitol. The design enables visitors to mark the transition from the Capitol to the open plaza. The two flanking pavilions are bridged to the fourth pavilion, which opens to the plaza. The architects designed this plaza to serve as a theater for the large-scale open-wire globe that encloses a neon Coca-Cola sign. Flags of 258 countries hang from the central atrium, giving visual expression to the truly global reach of the Coca-Cola Company.

Videos and interactive displays are incorporated into the rooms' colorful spaces with an informal ambience, and the design leads visitors on a linear path through the exhibits. Visitors make their way from one pavilion to the other, from cube to cube, and floor to floor until the tour is concluded. The architects' eclectic design for the World of Coca-Cola Pavilion transforms classical elements, such as columns and cornices with Coca-Cola imagery, creating a "best of both worlds" experience. This design realizes traditional and contemporary ideas about architecture, as it reinforces Coca-Cola's image as a worldwide product. Visitors can enjoy the site's freewheeling, but also focused, inventiveness.

At the main entrance, a revolving neon-lit advertising sign in the form of a globe refers to the global presence of Coca-Cola's product and the theme of the museum.

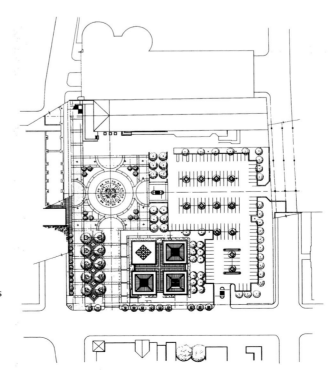

Site plan
The Coca-Cola plaza serves as the forecourt to the World of Coca-Cola pavilion and links the pavilion to the adjacent historic freight depot and Underground Atlanta.

Visitors to the World of Coca-Cola are drawn to the building through the open entry pavilion.

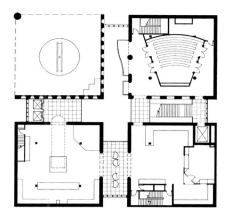

Third floor

Second floor

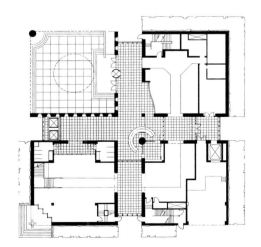

Ground floor

The widely recognized shape of the Coca-Cola bottle is used as a column support and is creatively lit for night visibility.

Rows of international flags are suspended from the skylight in the atrium, reinforcing the international presence of Coca-Cola while diffusing the natural sunlight.

Circulation through the exhibit pavilion occurs in the cross-shaped, sky-lit atrium.

Promenade Two, TVS Offices

Atlanta, Georgia 1990

Promenade Two is the second structure of a three million-square-foot mixed use development that was planned in three phases for a prominent site in midtown Atlanta at Peachtree Street between Fourteenth and Fifteenth Streets. For this project, TVS provided masterplanning and complete architectural services. The plan incorporated the existing 12-floor Promenade One office building, AT&T's Southeast Regional Headquarters – also a TVS design – with three new high-rise office towers, a conference/theater facility, supporting retail space, and a 5,000-car parking garage. Completed in 1991, the 38-story Promenade Two office tower hosts additional offices for AT&T, as well as the offices of TVS on the 25th through the 28th floors.

The complex is designed around a lushly landscaped garden that functions as both a gathering place and a central focal point for the entire site. A crescent-shaped pedestrian arcade provides a covered connection between the parking structure and the tower lobby and gives the garden an intimate cloistered enclosure.

The stepped-pyramid atop the building creates a distinctive and memorable silhouette on the Atlanta skyline. The silhouette form was then used as the principal motif throughout the structure's architectural detailing, most notably in the main entrance and the open-air promenade structure at the base of the building.

The architectural detailing vocabulary, which terminates the pinnacle of Promenade Two, is recalled in the graduated silhouette of its loggia.

Lighting accentuates the upper levels at night. The neo-gothic spire element combines with the stepped-pyramid form of the structure to achieve balance and continuity.

The Promenade Two tower signals a new urban vocabulary for the city of Atlanta.

The monumental stair at Promenade Two's main entrance recalls the stepped motif of the building's silhouette with its geometric arches and overhangs.

Promenade Two is situated in the landscape garden at the southern end of the TVS master plan.

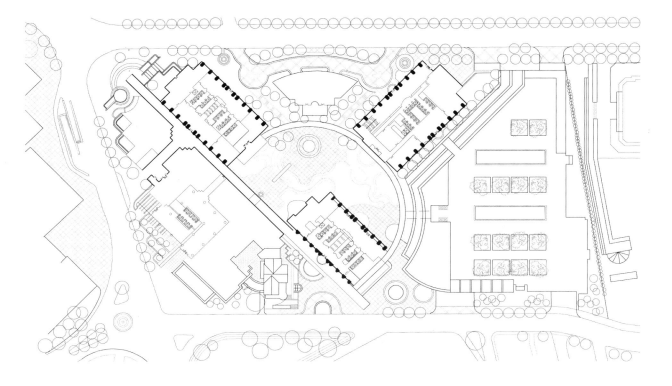

The TVS reception area incorporates light wood veneers, which ground the extended glass surfaces and serve as an appropriate backdrop for the firm's extensive glass art collection.

The 27th floor of the building houses TVS offices, including studio spaces, the primary reception area and conference rooms.

Tropical cherry wood flooring is used on the stair and in the halls throughout the multi-level offices.

The contrasting colors of the warm flooring and brightly-colored planar ceiling platforms accentuate the drama of the main hall perspective.

Concourse Complex and Towers

Atlanta, Georgia 1991

The Concourse Complex and Towers, developed by The Landmarks Group and Faison and Company, was master-planned by TVS as a multi-phased, 70-acre, mixed-use development. Located in northeast Atlanta, the complex was designed to accommodate sophisticated high-tech office and hotel facilities for corporate clients. The developers also hoped to create a "memorable shape on the horizon," reminiscent of classic urban high-rise construction. The completed Concourse Complex and Towers includes two low-rise office buildings, two mid-rise office buildings, two 32-floor office towers, a luxury 370-room Westin Hotel, a sporting club, and on-grade parking facilities.

For this complicated project, the TVS architects organized and designed the various architectural elements and building programs around a man-made central lake and lushly landscaped grounds. The low- and mid-rise office buildings were clustered in L-shaped pairs and designed to host atriums in their conjunctions. The architects then enhanced these spaces by placing multi-level glass walls on one side of each building. These dramatic garden-like atriums, featuring completely enclosed, environmentally-controlled gardens and accented with dining areas, were intended to soften the transition between interior and exterior spaces. In order to unify the various architectural masses and create aesthetic continuity, the architects established a basic design vocabulary that incorporates horizontal lines coupled with curved, banded glass. The use of a custom curtainwall on all buildings helped imbue the complex with a sense of place. To further promote this notion, the architects connected all of the facilities with a covered, tree-lined pedestrian concourse.

The clean, crisp, sculptural quality of the painted cast-in-place and pre-cast concrete members, accompanied by glazed screen walls, presents a striking impression on the skyline that clearly speaks of a cohesive community of buildings.

The towers' unique sculptural tops are a visual landmark for the development.

The complex is unified by its natural garden-like site, including a man-made central lake and lush landscaped grounds.

Masterplan

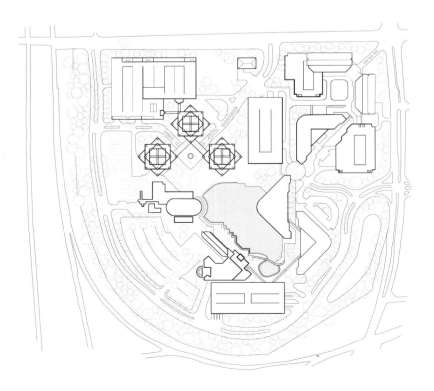

On the building's façade, a custom curtainwall and banded glass create horizontal lines and transitions, tying together all the buildings in the complex.

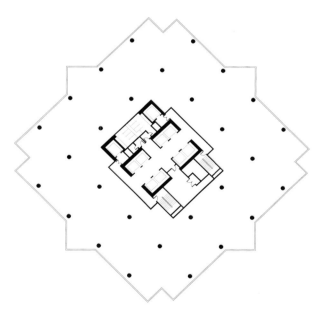

Typical Tower floor plan

The pre-cast concrete at the towerbase encases the reflective façade of the office building, which mirrors the sky.

Lobbies are envisioned as temperate natural environments, with tiled patio seating areas. Suspended geometric forms suggest movement as they cascade down from the ceiling.

Developing Atlanta's Convention District: TVS's Role

TVS has been a significant force in the creation and expansion of the congress center district, which has helped revitalize downtown Atlanta. The convention center has been a major economic engine for Atlanta and the state of Georgia for the past three decades. The entire complex, composed of various TVS-designed projects occupies 130 acres. The development began in 1967, when Tom Cousins, a leading Atlanta-based developer, leased railroad air-rights property from the state of Georgia. First on the agenda was a 2000-car parking structure that would help to catalyze the development of many

other facilities to come.

A market study indicated that an arena housing professional basketball and hockey teams would attract 2 million attendees, anchor the west end of the site, and expand the center of downtown Atlanta. In 1970, Cousins selected TVS to design the arena on a tight air-rights site between two viaducts and two railway lines, and adjacent to the city's incinerator. The incinerator closed, and the Omni arena opened to full house crowds in the fall of 1972.

This arena stimulated the development of the TVS-designed Omni International, a mixed-use

complex with 200,000 square feet of retail space, a 75,000-square-foot family entertainment pavilion, 600,000-square-feet of office space, and a 550-room luxury hotel, all housed in one building. Eventually, this facility would be bought by Ted Turner and turned into the headquarters and studios for CNN, the Cable News Network. Today, half a million visitors tour the CNN studios each year.

In 1973, the state of Georgia was searching for an appropriate site for a convention/trade show facility. Cousins offered to donate the property on the north side of Omni

Since 1970, TVS has been an integral force in shaping Atlanta's convention district.

International. The state agreed and selected TVS to design the 750,000-square-foot facility. The fast-track design/build process was completed in 26 months allowing the facility to open for a major show in September 1976. The phenomenal success of the Georgia World Congress Center stimulated a major expansion in 1986, which doubled its size. The state once again selected TVS to design the expansion, the largest building contract in the state's history. Indications of future expansions generated master planning by TVS for future phases of construction to the north and west of Phase II. TVS was later selected to

design the Phase III addition, bringing the total exhibition space to 1,000,000 square feet. In 2002, Phase IV of the facility will open, bringing the total exhibition area to more than 1,400,000 square feet in a complex of over 3.5 million square feet. The Phase IV expansion is located west of the existing building, and north of the Georgia Dome.

The state's decision to build a new domed stadium was a response to a need for a state-of-the-art stadium for the Atlanta Falcons National Football League team. TVS was part of the design team that created the 70,000-seat domed structure, which is linked

to the Georgia World Congress Center. The Georgia Dome opened in 1992.

When Atlanta was selected as the site for the 1996 summer Olympics, nine out of the nineteen venues used for the event were TVS-designed structures, including the Georgia Dome, Omni Arena and the Georgia World Congress Center. TVS was also selected to design Georgia International Plaza as a forecourt to the Georgia Dome and the Georgia World Congress Center. This plaza served as a gathering place between the Olympic venues and continues to serve Atlanta as a carefully designed, verdant, outdoor space.

Georgia Dome

Atlanta, Georgia 1992

The Georgia Dome, in conjunction with the Georgia World Congress Center, comprises one of the largest sports, entertainment, and convention complexes in the world. The domed multi-purpose facility hosted the Superbowl XXVIII in 1994, the gymnastics and basketball competitions for the 1996 Olympic games, as well as Superbowl XXXIV in 2000. The flexible dome functions as a sports stadium which hosts the Atlanta Falcons, a National Football League team. However, its careful design integrates the dramatic space with the adjacent convention center. TVS architects designed the interior spaces so that the artificial turf of the playing field could be removed and stored. The space can then be used as a 105,000-square-foot column-free exhibit area with an unlimited ceiling height and utilities similar to those provided in the floor of the adjacent Georgia World Congress Center.

The new facility was designed to establish direct pedestrian connections to the Georgia World Congress Center, the Omni Arena, and the Omni International Center, also known as CNN Center.

In addition, the expansion includes a 2,000-space parking deck.

As a sports stadium, the facility has the capacity to seat 70,700. The architects established a three-tiered seating concept. The tiers host, respectively, 27,500, 12,700, and 26,500 spectators. In addition to the spectator seating, a 250-seat press box and 203 private and corporate luxury suites were also incorporated into the facility. The suites just overlook the seating bowl and playing field on one side and a five-floor open atrium lobby on the opposite side. A combination of elevators, escalators, and pedestrian ramps were designed to provide access to seating and views of the facility.

A pedestrian concourse circulates around the oval-shaped plan, affording spectators unobstructed views across the playing field and easy access to seats, concessions and toilets. A distinctive tensegrity cable supported roof structure spans the 670-by-850-foot oval space. A 1/16- inch-thick translucent fiber glass reinforced fabric, coated with Teflon covers the structure permitting filtered daylight into the space and providing a sense of the outdoors.

The tensile structure of the Georgia Dome's cable-stayed roof blurs the boundaries between inside and outside by flooding the arena with natural daylight.

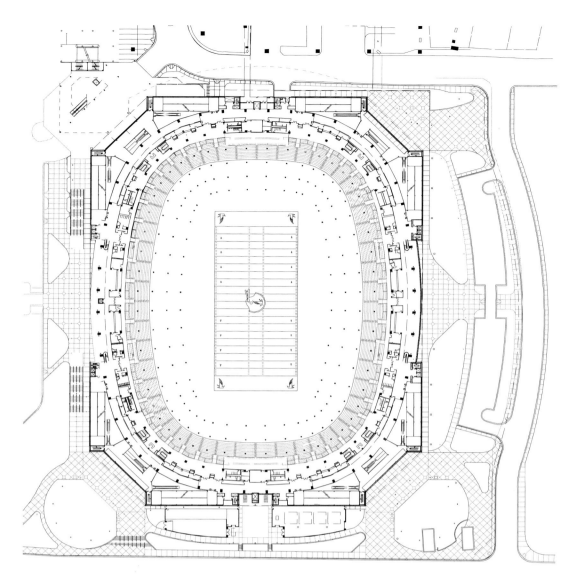

Mezzanine floor plan

The Georgia Dome, viewed
from afar, is an iconic
contribution to the Atlanta
cityscape.

Various circulation paths transverse the Georgia Dome's five-floor open atria, facilitating way-finding in the stadium.

Café seating and a collection of cheerfully colored flags line the interior of the glass curtainwall in one of the Dome's light-filled atria.

Georgia World Congress Center

Atlanta, Georgia 1993

Since its original opening in 1976, the remarkable success of the Georgia World Congress Center has necessitated three expansions. Through careful planning and design of the center, the architects took a marginal area adjacent to a warehouse district and revitalized it into a vibrant center that houses conventions, sports facilities, and a hotel. TVS has provided master planning, programming, and architectural design for all phases of the center. Each expansion has incorporated architectural elements, which are similar to the original design, while introducing new design themes and exploring new qualities.

The Phase III expansion of the Georgia World Congress Center convention facility added a total of 580,000 square feet, which included 330,000 square feet of exhibit space, six new meeting rooms, and a 400-seat restaurant. The architects understood the necessity of maintaining a sense of continuity throughout the Congress Center, so their scheme does not disrupt the existing exhibition hall. While introducing new themes and exploring different spatial qualities that would enhance the existing architectural vocabulary, the architects enlivened the center with daylight, articulated and diversified spatial range, and provided greater accessibility to the outdoor spaces and gardens. Public circulation spaces with related support and service areas were also established, and the original concourse was extended to provide access for the new entry points.

TVS, along with Heery International, is currently designing the Phase IV expansion of the center. The program consists of 420,000 square feet of new exhibit space, a 45,000-square-foot ballroom, 75,000 square feet of meeting space, and generous public circulation space for registration and pre-function activities. This expansion will give the Congress Center/Georgia Dome close to 1.5 million square feet of exibit space.

Located to the west of the existing facility with major frontage along Northside Drive, the site for this expansion provides space for ample vehicular drop-off, strengthens the relationship to the Dome, and creates a new presence for the Congress Center within the city. Phase IV is also an opportunity to centralize certain functions and organize spaces that complement the Center, the Dome, and nearby Centennial Olympic Park.

TVS is exploring exterior enhancements, which will unify the existing building with the Phase IV expansion. Construction is underway with a completion date in 2002.

The long expanse of clerestory windows provides a light-filled interior at the upper concourse.

The steel structure creates a dramatic entrance into the building's lobby. Direct and reflected light, the latticework of the steel above, and a strongly patterned floor create a powerful composition.

The expansive concourse is organized and enriched by custom carpeting. Rectangular grids are suspended from the ceiling, diffusing natural light.

46

The Phase IV expansion will include a dramatic grand concourse opening off of an entry plaza that connects to the Georgia Dome.

Ground floor plan.

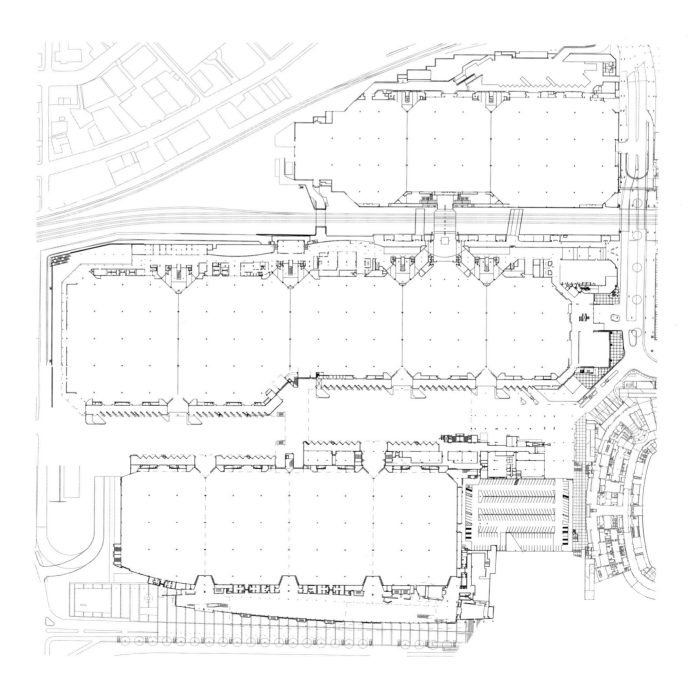

A multi-dimensional space is created with fountains, monoliths, and decorative pools of water.

The recessed food service area is highlighted by neon signage.

Convention goers are served by generous circulation zones that integrate the multiple expansion phases and encourage movement throughout the space.

The exhibit halls provide a neutral backdrop for creative convention planners.

Georgia International Plaza

Atlanta, Georgia 1996

Georgia International Plaza is a seven-acre public plaza located in downtown Atlanta. It serves as a pedestrian gathering space, as well as a forecourt to the Georgia World Congress Center, the Georgia Dome, and the Philips Arena Complex. Designed as a visitor destination for the 1996 Olympic Games, the plaza unifies the complex and connects the three facilities with public transportation. The architects established paths throughout the plaza that link various components of the complex to an adjacent MARTA (Metropolitan Atlanta Rapid Transit Authority) rail station. The plaza stands atop an existing 1,000-car parking facility, to which the architects added another 1,000-car parking deck.

The design is dominated by sixteen 70-foot-tall light towers, which are arranged in a grid. Spaced 110 feet on center, they provide all the lighting for the plaza. Using these towers, the TVS team defined a central area of the plaza and created a focal point for pedestrian activity. The plaza is composed of large grass fields, fountains, and intimate tree-shaded gardens.

To the south, a gently sloping lawn connects the plaza with the intersection of International Boulevard and Techwood Drive. The design also features a monumental cascading stair that leads to the parking levels below and brings light into the lower levels. The architects chose design elements, such as the light towers, the green spaces, and the great stair, which orient arriving visitors and create a human scale that was needed to convert this enormous rooftop into a vital urban plaza. By linking parking facilities with the landscaped plaza, this project sets a precedent for public space in future air-rights developments.

The grid of 20-foot-tall light towers creatively illuminates the plaza and provides visual interest for pedestrians.

Light columns constructed of translucent glass and steel panels, create a processional path from the parking to the monumental plaza.

The dramatically lit plaza was a popular gathering place during the 1996 Olympic Games.

A dramatic and colorful slot brings light to all nine levels of the parking deck below the plaza.

The grid of light towers is used to create primary pedestrian throughways.

The sculpture commemorates the 1996 Olympics and serves as a focal point for the International Plaza.

Phipps Plaza

Atlanta, Georgia 1992

TVS understands that retail spaces and shopping centers serve the social and commercial needs of communities. Because they are sensitive to context, TVS designers have created centers of commerce that, in many cases, serve as new town centers.

Some designs require extravagant detailing and an elegant touch in order to relate to the visitors. For the renovation and expansion of Phipps Plaza in Atlanta, Georgia, TVS conceived a highly articulated and richly appointed design, which responded to the owner's desire for a space that combined the grand and ceremonial with the warm and intimate. Two primary spaces are featured. The "Court of the South" highlights the region's gracious heritage with a grand double-spiral staircase and a gold-leafed ceiling with a crystal chandelier. In contrast, the volume and detailing of the three-story "Monarch Court," with its magnificent oval skylight, reflects the modern energy and excitement of Atlanta and the New South. The 120,000-square-foot public mall area features the warmth of American black cherry detailing, hand-cast solid bronze stanchions at railings, and 16 different marble floor patterns. The detailing of each of the center's three main concourses is inspired by local flora: the Magnolia, the Dogwood, and the Camellia.

The exterior utilizes warm-toned brick and pre-cast concrete on the primary façade, portraying a friendly and inviting, yet stable and permanent impression to the public.

The new Monarch Court is highlighted by a marble medallion of overlapping geometric patterns on the floor, as well as an elliptical skylight.

American Black Cherry is a
featured finish throughout the
mall, while the open rails on
balconies and stairs feature
double-sided, hand-cast
bronze stanchions that
symbolize a flower seed, stem,
leaves, and bud.

The columns allude to the classical architecture of the old south.

The elliptical skylight dramatically highlights the three-level Monarch Court.

Mobile Convention Center

Mobile, Alabama 1993

The new Mobile Convention Center sits on a prominent riverfront site at the end of Government Street, one of the city's most important thoroughfares. Prior to its development, a feasibility study established that such a facility required 100,000 square feet of exhibition space and 40,000 square feet of meeting and ballroom facilities to accommodate the city's convention and trade show market. Working with associate architects, The Architect's Group, TVS provided programming and design services for the new facility. Their scheme respects the contextual constraints of the surrounding urban environment while incorporating those architectural elements, such as the white façades and green roofs, that are typical of traditional Mobile architecture.

The design solution addressed the prominent riverfront site by providing and encouraging public access to the waterfront and establishing an architectural space to enhance public activity. Based on an understanding of the site, the architects developed a program to create a visual and physical connection between the neighboring downtown area and the new convention center. To underscore the convention center's importance, they designed a public entrance beacon, capped by a tall tower that is a landmark at night, reminiscent of waterfront lighthouse structures. In order to improve access and facilitate at-grade crossings at the heavily trafficked intersection, the architects incorporated a pedestrian bridge from the adjacent hotel and parking structure and a public entrance plaza into the total plan. The plaza, along the southern façade of the building, provides direct public access to the riverfront and serves as a transition between the convention center and the riverfront park.

Oriented toward the waterfront, the building provides access to the city's "riverwalk" and increases the importance of the downtown location. Built like a traditional veranda, one-third of the 590,000-square-foot convention center sits upon a base of pre-cast concrete pilings that lift it above the flood plane and make way for two CSX rail lines below. The remainder of the building sits on concrete pressure-injected footings. Following this form, deep overhangs surround the building on three sides in a manner reminiscent of the area's traditional architecture. For the building's outdoor spaces, the architects used recovered nineteenth-century waterfront street pavers at all water-wall and river-edge fountains. By using materials and forms that were already part of the city's architectural heritage, the architects tied the convention center to Mobile's other public buildings.

The architects also oriented the interior components of the facility toward the waterfront. Both the ballroom and the exhibit hall feature outdoor decks and concession seating areas, which provide visual and physical access to the riverwalk activity below. The interior spaces are dominated by an exposed roof-framing system. In the exhibition hall, the architects incorporated an exposed 150-by-150-foot, two-way pipe truss with 30-foot bays, which cantilever from the perimeter. The roofs of the ballroom and the meeting rooms are concealed steel trusses with long-span joists. The design vocabulary for the interior partitions also emphasizes structure. White, scored, split-faced masonry units are used for the interior concourse walls, and smooth white units accent meeting room entrances. The meeting room interiors are constructed of light rose, split-faced units.

The concourses also feature exposed steel fan trusses borrowed from the old courthouse design, as the architects carried this notion of structure throughout the facility. Glass-block clerestory windows running around the public concourses provide a continuous band of diffuse light in this area. These concourses feature gable roofs constructed of exposed steel trusses infilled with white-washed Southern pine decking. An exterior staircase cascades down from the elevated concourse to open the building to the public and activate the center's façade.

In its first year of operation, attendance at trade shows and conventions boosted the city's revenues by $100 million. As a result, the center has become the cornerstone in the evolution of Mobile's waterfront. Furthermore, it's become a historical marker for the city, reminding visitors and residents alike of the city's history as a seaport.

The highly visible tower functions as a landmark in the surrounding downtown neighborhood.

61

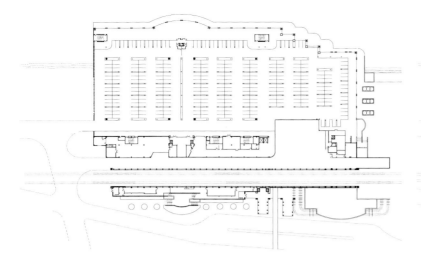

Parking Level, ground floor

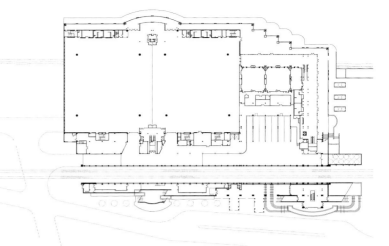

Exhibit Hall, second floor

A rhythmic succession of bays lines the façade of the Mobile Convention Center, incorporating the traditional form of a veranda into its exterior concourse.

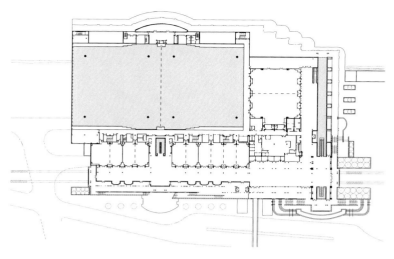

Meeting Rooms, third floor

Lighting fixtures that recall antique marine lamps ring the perimeter of the center, while spotlights are utilized to identify pedestrian paths. The floodlit tower is the monumental focus of the site.

The concourse roof features wood decking on steel fan trusses, a reference to Mobile's traditional architecture.

Human-scaled fenestration patterns and glass block clerestory windows allow sunlight to permeate the Mobile Convention Center's public pre-function spaces.

King of Prussia

King of Prussia, outside Philadelphia, Pennsylvania, is the second largest retail complex in the United States, with 2.9 million square feet of retail area. The master plan for the Plaza and the Court at King of Prussia utilizes a unique series of spaces that define the project and orient the visitor. The TVS team placed a series of circular plazas and courts along the pedestrian walkways within the complex. These walkways are enclosed in glass and recall the arcades of urban commercial centers of the past. The walkways are broken down into city blocks, with plazas or courts located at block intersections. Special colored-glass skylights, light fixtures, flooring patterns, and color palettes give each of these spaces a distinct character.

The central meeting place is located at the approximate geometric center of the complex. The café court has a distinctive design, which encapsulates the elegance of the overall plan. Designed as an outdoor courtyard, the central plaza is woven with patterned cobblestone paths. An ornamental fountain and seating encourage public congregation. A cathedral-like colored-glass skylight covers the entire area. Steel balconies reflect outdoor verandas.

The TVS team used steel and metal detailing on towers and balconies of the King of Prussia complex to embody the classic architectural style of Philadelphia. These details are balanced with the patterns and colors prevalent in the surrounding Pennsylvania Dutch countryside. Flooring patterns and handrail details were chosen to reinforce the connection of the complex to the context in which it was built.

Ornamental metalwork, dramatic lighting, and elegant marble flooring combine to provide texture and a feeling of elegance.

A distinctive architectural style, different from the rest of the mall, gives the Café Court a special sense of place.

Along the perimeter of the arcade, the detailing recalls the look and feel of an exterior building façade.

Multi-colored glass, combined in an elaborate pattern, creates a memorable Tiffany shade ceiling above the Café Court.

Ornamental metalwork detailing carries into the surroundings of each distinctive court.

A dramatic fountain creates a focal point for the garden plaza in the center of the Café Court.

Long Beach
Convention Center

Long Beach, California 1994

TVS architects were commissioned to establish a new identity for the Long Beach Convention Center. The facility had to meet the community's trade exhibition needs and animate an aging, elevated, pedestrian promenade, which was constructed to connect the downtown business sector to the waterfront retail area. Through an architectural program that included renovation, expansion, and modernization, the architects established the convention center as a vital part of the downtown urban fabric. The center stretches from the restaurant district to a new marina and retail neighborhood at the waterfront and has transformed the previously desolate promenade into an active public piazza.

The central challenge of the construction process required that the existing convention center and several nearby facilities, including a 500-room hotel, 4,000-seat auditorium, and12,000-seat arena, remain operational during the construction period. In addition, the centrally located mechanical plant serving all these facilities had to be replaced without interrupting services.

The limitations of the site made it necessary to locate the expansion atop an existing 750-car parking structure. The architects took advantage of the elevated position by creating a grand glazed concourse that stretches along the length of the existing pedestrian promenade, anchored on the north by downtown Long Beach and on the south by a 500-room hotel. The glazing provides pedestrians with an animated view of the activities within. Inside the concourse, the architects located meeting facilities on two levels, providing conventioneers with panoramic views of the harbor, the Queen Mary, and the Palos Verdes Mountains along the sea.

The architects also believed it appropriate to create a ceremonial entrance to the convention center. For this area, TVS designed a grand staircase flanked by two elevator towers with sculptural, glazed light fixtures at their tops. In the day, the towers' softly ridged bases and flared, green-tinted glass tops speak to the tall palm trees nearby, unifying the built structure with the natural environment. In the evening, the lighted towers call visitors to the entrance, and the glowing concourse functions as a landmark for downtown Long Beach.

At night, the concourse is internally lit, so that it appears as an extended column of light.

The convention center's long pedestrian promenade extends from the downtown area to the newly created entertainment district at the marina.

Ballroom level plan

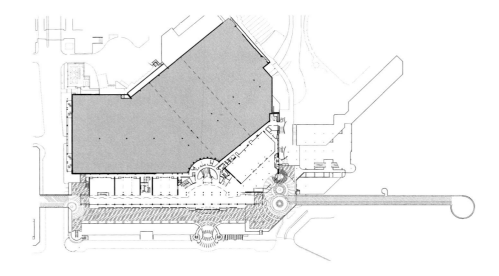

The abstracted wave design of the carpet recalls the staccato series of linear steel arches.

The scaled texture applied to this wall recalls the convention center's link with the oceanfront and the marine surroundings.

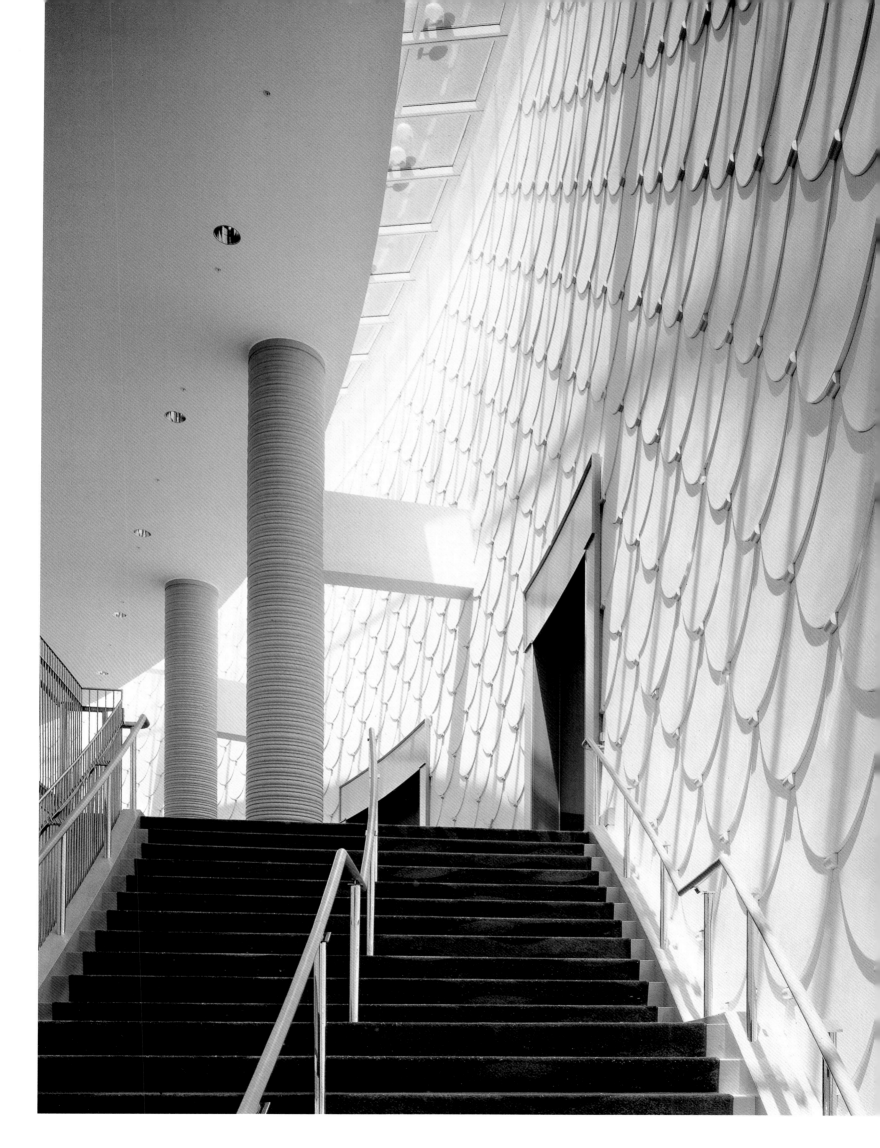

The bow windows, intricate
glazing patterns, clerestories
and distinctive entry portals
used on the carefully
articulated façade humanize
the scale of the monumental
building.

Pennsylvania Convention Center

Philadelphia, Pennsylvania 1994

The Pennsylvania Convention Center Authority wanted to minimize the problematic aspects of placing the convention center in the middle of the city while maximizing its potential to revitalize a downtown area nearly shadowed by William Penn's statue high atop City Hall. In response to these wishes, TVS architects created a facility encompassing 1.3 million square feet which they carefully integrated into the historic urban fabric of Philadelphia.

The convention center's exhibition building houses 440,000 square feet of exhibit halls, 60,000 square feet of meeting rooms, and the major support and service spaces for the entire facility. It is constructed of poured-in-place reinforced concrete, with a steel roof structure and deck. The main exhibition floor is approximately 25 feet above street level; this places 300,000 square feet of contiguous, but divisible, exhibit hall space at the same height as the former platform level of the adjacent train shed. Its 27-bay loading dock, on the same elevated level, can be reached by a nearby expressway access road. Thus the major convention trucks service and loading/unloading functions are separated both visually and functionally from the busy grid of the street. The exhibition building spans a main north-south arterial street, which bisects its site, forms primary frontage for the train shed, and creates a block-long drop-off corridor for buses and taxis beneath the building. The primary entrances into the facility flank the key intersection of this north-south artery and the major street that fronts the concourse.

TVS architects were faced with the challenge of integrating the convention center into the physical fabric and scale of the city. They met the challenge with composed and articulated façades that incorporate granite, limestone, and brick, all materials common to the historic architecture of the city. Distinctive entry portals, clerestories, canopies, and bow windows overlay façades, which are organized in a series of bays to recall the rhythm of historic building fronts throughout Philadelphia. The façades facing each of the four main adjacent streets present a composition of materials and building elements that addresses the scale and character of each specific frontage.

A continuous multi-leveled circulation concourse fronts the south side of the upper level exhibition halls. Bays of limestone-clad columns and generous expanses of window formally articulate its façade. The barrel vaults of the exhibition hall roof recall the barrel vaults of the train shed in a subdued and respectful manner. A continuous skylight and transverse dormers open up the linear roof and reinforce the rhythm of the bays on the façade. Bow windows, which can be closed with operable partitions when necessary, not only animate the exterior façade, but also provide daylight and city views to the interior spaces of the exhibit halls. Interior and exterior lighting emphasizes glass-enclosed stair towers at both ends and above the central intersection, and works to restore a sense of vitality and security to a once-decaying commercial district.

The architects transformed the train shed into a major entry point for the facility. Their design aligned the main floor level of the convention center with the floor of the train shed, approximately 25 feet above street level, allowing all major streets in the area to remain open. A new multi-level bridge connects the train shed to the exhibition hall. The bridge houses a registration concourse that serves both buildings, a multi-vendor food service facility, and the banquet kitchen for the ballroom in the train shed. A majestic 50,000-square-foot grand hall preserves the 90-foot ceiling height and 260-foot floor width of the original shed structure. The floor of the grand hall is finished in boldly patterned terrazzo and accented with marble and stainless steel inlays, which recall the placement and pattern of the original 10 sets of railway tracks that once carried commuter trains into and out of the city. The original cast-iron structural elements of the shed are exposed throughout the grand hall and

ballroom in the train shed.

The transition from the grand hall to the ballroom, one level above, is handled by a series of formal marble-clad terraces that integrate escalators, elevators, reception areas, and a paired grand stairway flanked by signature light fixtures designed by the architects. The ballroom, open to the historic structure and the roof deck above, is lit by a suspended grid supporting both indirect and direct light sources, which together provide for a wide variety of lighting programs to suit the mood and character of a given event. The ballroom is separated acoustically from the grand hall by a full-height glass partition, the mullion pattern and spacing of which echo the existing shed's historical glass curtainwall.

The main goal of the design was to create an atmosphere of hospitality and quality within an efficiently functioning facility, appropriate to the standards of a continually evolving convention and meetings market. The facility has stimulated the continuing revitalization of a district that had, in recent years, fallen behind other areas of the city in its pace of positive growth and redevelopment. The renovation and adaptive reuse of the train shed keeps existing building fabric intact and establishes a lively public market place at the street level directly below. The market is one of the city's treasured cultural landmarks; it was renovated, without ever completely closing down, during the construction of this convention center.

Studies are currently underway for an expansion of the Philadelphia Convention Center, attesting to the enormous success it has experienced. The Center received the AIA Honor Award for Urban Design in the year 2000.

A multi-level bridge spans the street and makes an appropriate connection between the historic train shed and the new convention facilities.

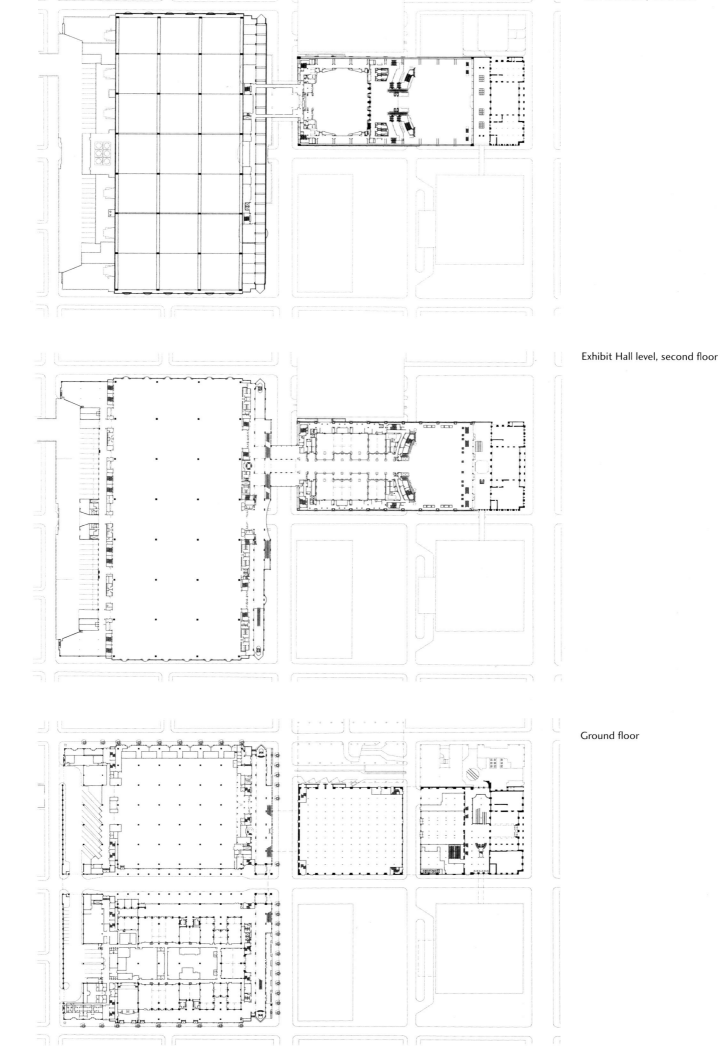

Ballroom level, third floor

Exhibit Hall level, second floor

Ground floor

Monumental stairs and escalators lead to the pre-function space for the ballroom, which was constructed within the volume of the historic train shed.

Freestanding signature lighting pylons, designed by the architect, frame the perimeter of the train station.

The original trusses soar 90 feet above the grand hall. Inlayed stainless steel marks the locations of the tracks on the floor of the trainshed.

(following page) The ballroom takes advantage of the original roof structure to create a unique space. The custom designed carpet brings an appropriate level of elegance to the ballroom.

A sculptured stair that connects all levels accents the light and airy atrium, which links the three levels of the concourse.

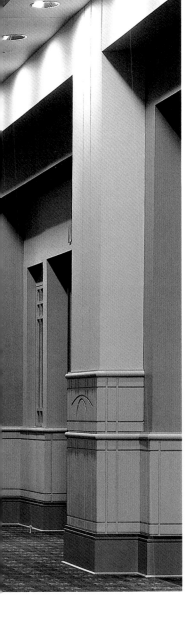

Mei Ling Horn's "China Wedge" sculpture is a special point of interest for the center's visitors.

The refined elegance of the center's architecture provides an ideal backdrop for an extensive art collection, including this portrait by Susan Moore.

Charlotte Convention Center

Charlotte, North Carolina 1995

When TVS initiated the design work for the Charlotte Convention Center, they quickly realized that the three-block site located in Charlotte's Uptown district was very small, making it difficult to accommodate the building program desired by the city. The three city blocks were configured in an L-shape with one block separated from the other two by a railroad right-of-way, which was to be maintained for a future light rail system that would eventually make a stop at the facility.

Because much of Charlotte's built environment, like that of many sunbelt cities, had been recently constructed, existing architecture did not provide the architects with a strong historic design vocabulary upon which to expand. The clients still preferred traditional imagery, while they also saw Charlotte as an emerging and progressive force and believed that the convention center should be at the center of this growth. The resulting TVS design provided a balance between this contemporary vision and an orientation toward traditional architectural style.

The complexities of the convention center's site demanded that the functions be stacked vertically. The 275,000-square-foot exhibition hall was placed

Custom designed carpet patterns allude to the intricate detailing of handcrafted textile designs.

The oculus in the great hall houses a sculpture by Jamie Carpenter. The opening becomes a radiant lantern in the evening, seen from Charlotte's city streets.

on the lower level, creating contiguous exibit space that easily accomodates the 350 pounds-per-square-foot floor load. This design also allowed large vehicles servicing the exhibit halls to enter at the lower end of the site and move to the loading docks. Because the architects covered the loading docks with the upper floors, they were able to conceal from view this traditionally troublesome aesthetic aspect of convention center design. This allowed them to incorporate major public circulation concourses, identified by a vaulted roof structure, which provided clear access to the exhibit halls, meeting rooms, and the ballroom. They positioned these elements parallel to the adjacent streets, creating intersecting axes that meet in a grand central hall that serves as a meeting point in the center of the building. The architects crowned the great hall with a large skylight above an

oculus. This distinctive architectural element is visible from Tryon, Charlotte's main street, and becomes a land mark lantern at night.

The TVS design for the convention center utilizes a modern vocabulary that relies on traditional principles of permanence, scale, and detail. The architects chose to use massive forms to create a sense of civic dignity, but their juxtaposition of these forms is dynamic rather than symmetrical. Alluding to more traditional materials, the architects used limestone-colored precast concrete on the building's exterior and gray metal cladding for the concourse vault. Internally, TVS chose primary colors as contemporary accents. In the public spaces, the architects incorporated a custom carpet designed with intricate details suggestive of handcrafted textiles. Such details provide the space with a sense of intimacy.

The rhythmic composition of the exterior façade is terminated by an artfully designed main entrance with a vaulted roof structure.

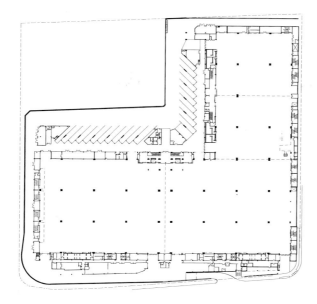

Exhibit Hall level, ground floor

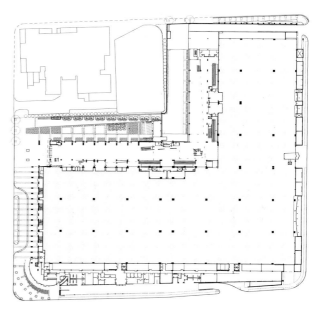

Entry level, second floor

Meeting Room level, third floor

(following pages)
The interior concourse serves
as a meeting point and
provides clear circulation to the
exhibit hall, ballroom, and
meeting rooms.

United Parcel Service World Headquarters

Atlanta, Georgia 1995

United Parcel Service (UPS) commissioned TVS to plan and design its world headquarters on a heavily wooded 35-acre site. The structure, meant to establish a productive work environment and encourage interaction between individuals and functional groups, comprises more than 600,000 square feet, including office and support areas for approximately 2,000 employees, a 621-seat cafeteria, central conference and training facilities, and a company gallery. The plan also incorporates parking for more than 1,800 automobiles, with two structural parking decks.

The architects' design responds to this program and creates harmony between the space of the built environment and the natural beauty of the surrounding landscape. Special care was taken to preserve the site and engage it in a reciprocal relationship with the structural components of the design. In addition to furnishing a complete architectural and engineering design, TVS's responsibilities included land-use, master-planning, and interior architecture.

The building was designed to have minimal impact on the steeply sloped site. Trees as close as 15 feet from the face of the building were saved, and an existing stream became the focal point of the built environment. The architects designed two seven-story structures, one on each side of the stream, and connected them with a bridge. The design utilized the space of the bridge for a continuous four-story pedestrian gallery, the cafeteria, a conference center, executive offices, and a roof garden. By designing a structure that was permeable to its natural site, the architects created a facility that enables employees to enjoy the site throughout the day.

TVS took great pains to provide natural light and exterior views to all employees. The design capitalized on the transparent building's ability to reflect the woodland setting when making decisions about materials and finishes. Glass exterior walls were designed to extend to 10-foot-high ceilings, allowing natural light to penetrate all workstations, and make the division between inside and outside even less distinguishable. In the private offices, organized around the core of the building, the architects featured clerestory glass around the full perimeter of the offices, providing light and outside views across the width of the building. The geometrical light fixtures, furniture, and graphics were designed to offer visual contrasts throughout the public spaces. The architects chose a light, neutral palette. A range of paints and fabric wall coverings complemented by clear-finished Honduras mahogany trim, Makore, and Sapele wood veneers served to further emphasize the natural properties of the constructed space.

The corporate art collection, a mix of contemporary art and native crafts and textiles, represents the many cultures of the UPS family and customers around the globe. The collection is distributed throughout the facility and underscores the architects' democratic organization of the entire plan.

Pre-cast concrete beams are positioned off of the main structure, providing sun shading while allowing for views of the landscape.

95

The formal building entrance is oriented off of the circular automobile drop-off.

Two seven-story towers are carefully sited to preserve the natural landscape; a four-story bridge, which spans an existing stream, links the towers.

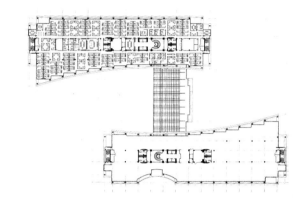

Typical floor plan

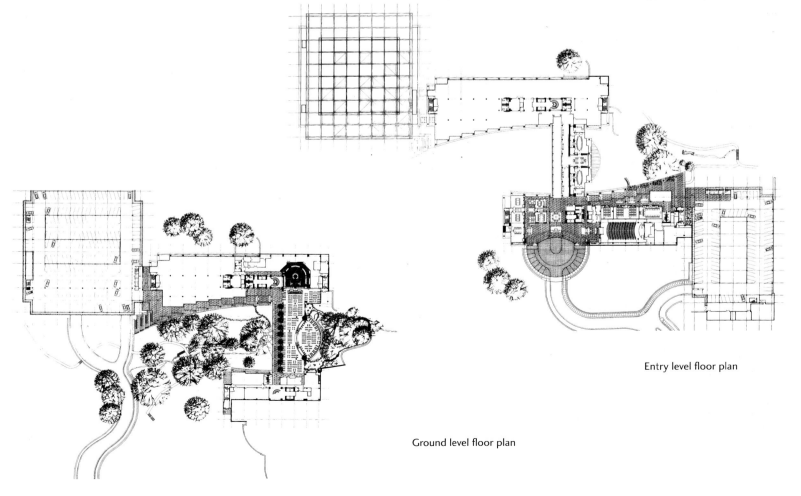

Entry level floor plan

Ground level floor plan

The bridge that links the two buildings includes the multi-level atrium, visually connecting the public space and the corporate offices.

Trees as close as fifteen feet to the building were preserved during construction, minimizing the impact of the building on the environment.

Permeable to natural light and views, the design enables employees to enjoy the site throughout the day.

The design for the lobby incorporates leather upholstered seating and wood tables, which organize the space. Mahogany paneling, built to accommodate the company's art collection, flanks the hall, which runs along the edge of the concourse.

The dining area underlines a grid motif with its flooring, divider walls, art work, and seating configuration.

The neutral palette of the interior provides an appropriate backdrop for the eclectic art collection.

(following page) Warm-colored wood and leather finishes enhance the contemporary conference facilities. The unique shape of the custom designed conference table is reflected in the design of the ceiling above.

(following page) A spiral staircase with strong geometry and skylight dramatically connects each level of the seven story towers.

Prince Street Technologies
Corporate Office

Cartersville, Georgia 1995

In the fall of 1994, Prince Street Technologies, an innovative supplier of high-end custom carpet, planned the construction of a 5.7-million-dollar manufacturing facility to house its corporate offices and showrooms on a 25-acre, landscaped site directly off State Highway 61 in Cartersville, Georgia. TVS won a design competition for the facility containing 160,000 square feet of manufacturing space, 15,000 square feet of office space, an 11,000-square-foot sample lab, a 5,000-square-foot showroom, and a 3,000-square-foot design studio. The arrangement of these spaces was expected to promote to the facility's visitors, many of whom are members of the design community, the notion that a corporate family exists at work.

TVS made teamwork central to its design with a plan that would create strong bonds between all employees sharing a workspace and reflect the collaborative nature of the relationship between Prince Street Technologies and its employees. The architects also concentrated on designing the offices and showroom to support the activities taking place within them. To this end, the architectural solution included Prince Street's product priorities: texture, pattern, color, and innovative carpet design.

Both employees and visitors enter the facility through the showroom, which surrounds the Custom Sample Lab. Here, both groups can mingle, while visitors await the start of guided tours.

A display of the company's products at the point of arrival is a continuous reminder that carpet quality and innovation is critical to the company success. The corporate offices leading from the showroom extend along the manufacturing sector, creating a connection between two separate business activities. The architects also scattered informal meeting areas throughout the space to further promote team interaction.

The offices are adjacent to the manufacturing plant and are separated by a glass wall, giving the office staff, technicians, and designers a visual as well as physical connection. In the plant, a large picture window offers workers a view to the changing textures and colors of the landscape. In response to the owner's environmental concerns, no irrigation or chemical fertilizers were used, and storm drainage was managed above ground.

The architects used simple unfinished materials, natural lighting and landscaping to create friendly spaces that are conducive to a cooperative work environment. The architects and interior designers chose low-maintenance finishes common in industrial architecture, but they arranged and detailed them in unique ways. The under-finished aesthetic allows the carpet product to stand out. The facility functions as a high-profile marketing space, while underscoring the primary components of the business.

Emerging from the glass façade, the main entrance is marked by a suspended overhang and a triangular metal tower fitted with louvers and spotlights.

The glass façade frames a
central, cylindrical, brick wall.

Glazed exterior openings with
translucent sunscreening
devices allow workers to enjoy
natural light and views of the
surrounding landscape.

All employees and visitors enter the building through the showroom, where new products are highlighted within the underfinished space.

Conference rooms are dispersed throughout the facility. Glass walls exhibit the soundproofed meeting spaces, while providing a degree of acoustical privacy.

The design studio, located above the showroom level, overlooks the manufacturing facility.

Salt Palace
Convention Center

Salt Lake City, Utah 1996

The original Salt Palace facilities, built in the 1960s, were out of date and required replacement with a state-of-the-art facility. Current and projected needs demanded new leasable space for exhibition, meeting, and banquet events, including a new 40,000-square-foot ballroom. The prominent site stretches along a major downtown artery, adjacent to the Temple Square of the Mormon Tabernacle, the arts center, and the symphony hall. The design needed to create new architectural imagery that would complement the adjacent cultural arts complex and also provide sidewalk animation for the length of two jumbo-sized city blocks. In addition, the new Salt Palace Convention Center needed a high-profile entrance that would serve as a visual landmark for pedestrians approaching the facility from nearby hotels.

TVS designed a 100-foot cylindrical tower to mark the mid-block main entrance to the convention center and, thus, provided a dramatic and elegant monument, visible from hotels many blocks away.

The architects designed the tower to exude authority over the urban landscape, but established its delightful personality with a latticework of structural members. This animated structure creates a delicate silhouette against the sky during the day and a fanciful lantern at night. The tower is joined by the rotunda-like visitors center, the new triangulated entrance to the art museum, and dynamic public artwork, consisting of five double-bladed windmills, which creates a necklace of urban charms that energizes 600 feet of frontage without overshadowing the cultural arts complex. A sculpture courtyard and a civic-scaled water feature add visual and artistic delight. The interior design includes a grand-scale concourse to serve the exhibit halls, the ballroom, and the meeting rooms. The TVS team configured the concourse so natural light would flood into the dramatic space created by high sculptural curved trusses. The exhibit hall, ballroom, and concourses were designed to accommodate easy future expansion.

Dynamic features, including a landmark tower and windmill structures, are incorporated into the design.

Windmill structures animate the façade at street level.

Devised as a new landmark for the city, a monumental tower marks the main entrance.

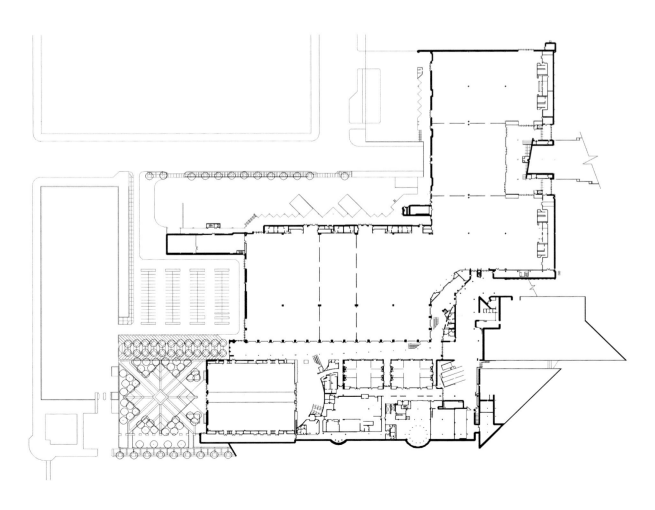

Exhibit Hall level

The structural steel latticework within the tower provides visual animation from within, as well as from afar.

The glass wall separating the interior and exterior space joins a sloping, steel, grid-supported wall. The mullions form a subtle patterned design.

Elegant, graceful, steel trusses extend the length of the concourse.

The rhythm of the overhead trusses is punctuated by regularly spaced openings and skylights on one wall, and shaped sconces on the opposite.

Woodruff Arts Center

Atlanta, Georgia 1996

Since its inception 27 years ago, the Woodruff Arts Center has been home to the Atlanta College of Art, the Alliance Theatre Company, the High Museum of Art, and the Atlanta Symphony. Located in midtown Atlanta on the critical spine of Peachtree Street, the center had grown significantly over the years. In 1990, the Long-Range Facilities Planning Committee conducted an analysis and recommended the immediate renovation of the center to be completed before the 1996 Summer Olympics. TVS was chosen to fulfill the committee's objectives to give the center a new inviting image. To do this, TVS decided to create a pedestrian-friendly vehicular drop-off and a new public space allowing the Peachtree Street entrance to link with the galleria serving the symphony and theatre halls;and theater halls: In addition, the infrastructure was refurbished and portions of the massive concrete façade, which enclosed the Arts Center, were opened.

TVS's design exceeded the committee's expectations. In addition to transforming the existing drive into a motor and pedestrian plaza, the architects converted the top level of a parking structure between the center and the High Museum into a courtyard garden to create a semi-public space for social functions and public events.

The interior renovation included a redesign of the galleria and lobbies of the symphony hall and refurbishment of the Alliance Theatre and the Atlanta College of Art library. The architects dramatically transformed the two-story, rectangular galleria by adding large windows at each end, flooding the space with light and creating views to the High Museum. They gave the second floor balcony a long, graceful curve and connected it to the ground floor with two, grand, marble staircases. Glass and stainless steel handrails maintain a transparent connection between the floors and animate the space.

TVS replaced much of the massive concrete façade with a new curtainwall. The architects cut extensive openings in the walls and bowed out interior spaces with softer gray porcelain panels more akin to the High Museum's white façade.

The completed renovations includes a number of spaces for the performing arts, including the 1,762-seat Symphony Hall Auditorium, the 860-seat Alliance Theater, the 421-seat Rich Auditorium, and the 315-seat Studio Theater. Other renovated space, totaling 90,000 square feet, includes parts of the Atlanta College of Art Library, a new public entrance, a ticket office, a restaurant, a members' lounge, and a conference room.

The inviting new entrance leads from the pedestrian-friendly drop-off to the galleria, serving the symphony and theatre halls.

Much of the Arts Center's massive concrete façade was opened, and replaced with glazed curtainwall.

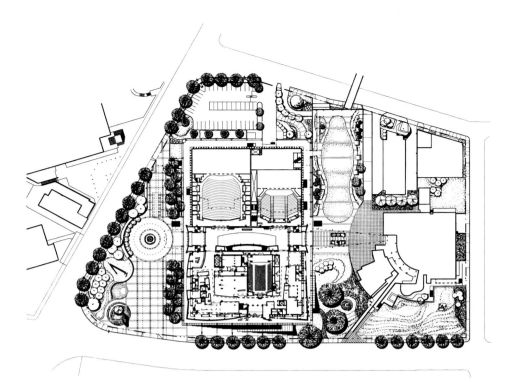

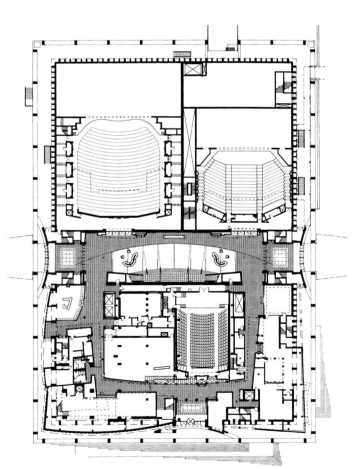

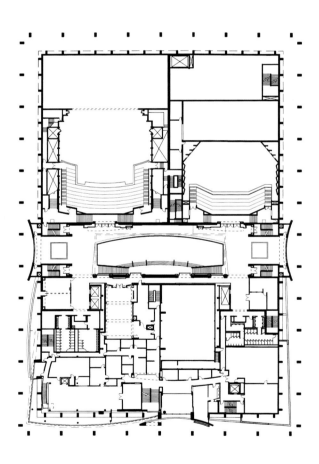

Site plan

Lobby floor plan

Second floor plan

The lobby combines marble flooring and carpeting which follow the form of the balcony. Stairs lead to a platform flanked by a wood paneled wall, and connect with the upper level.

adidas House
Southeast Regional Headquarters

Atlanta, Georgia 1996

adidas, one of the leading sports apparel and athletic shoe companies in the world, planned the renovation of seven adjacent warehouse buildings located on Marietta Street in downtown Atlanta. The 40,000-square-foot facility was used as the headquarters during the 1996 Olympic Games. After that event, the complex became adidas House Southeast Regional Headquarters and is now used during annual trade events, company meetings, and special events. Buildings One through Five contain adidas showrooms, offices, studios, and retail space. The last two buildings provide hospitality areas that

incorporate dining rooms, bars, lounges, and apartment lofts, as well as two levels of terraces that overlook the Centennial Olympic Park.

All aspects of the multi-use complex were designed to reflect the adidas image. TVS Interiors worked in conjunction with Smith Dalia Architects to decide on finishes and furnishings. The result was an industrial warehouse aesthetic. The interior spaces serve as a backdrop on which adidas can showcase products and highlight the spirit of past and present Olympic Games.

The industrial interior aesthetic of adidas House is punctuated by brightly-colored furniture.

Informal meeting spaces
incorporate the rustic elements
of exposed brick walls and
wood plank flooring, which
highlight contemporary
furnishings.

A wall mural in the lounge
illustrates the historical
background of the company
through a timeline and displays
vintage adidas merchandise.

Brick column cladding on lower floors falls away at the upper level, exposing more steel to reflect the project's industrial aesthetic.

Third floor plan

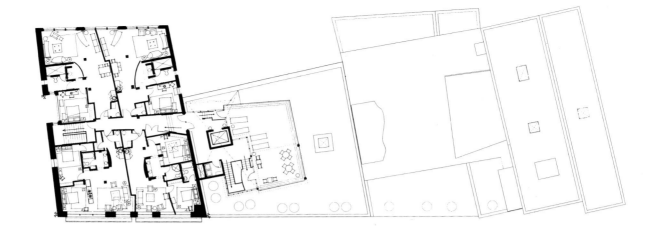

Second floor plan

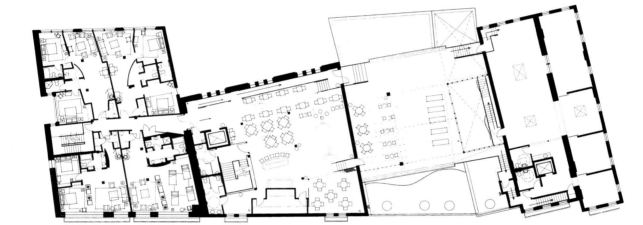

First floor plan

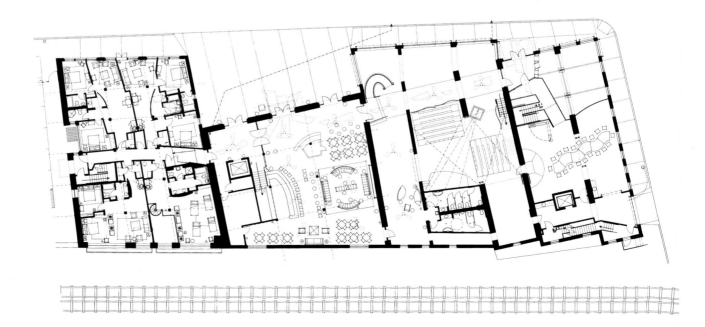

Individual showrooms feature sliding window frame doors, which provide privacy.

Beneath the neon-lit adidas logo, the bar provides a relaxed venue for entertaining clients.

Orange County Convention Center

Orlando, Florida 1996

The Orange County Convention Center located near Orlando, Florida, between Disney World and Universal Studios, has gone through several phases of renovation and expansion. TVS was commissioned by the Orange County Convention Center to establish guidelines for the Phases III and IV expansion of the facility and to complete the design of Phase III with the Orlando firm, Hunton, Brady, Pryor & Maso. The master plan provided for a total of 1.5 million square feet of exhibition space, a 60,000-square-foot ballroom, a 2,800-seat state-of-the-art auditorium, and an 800-seat lecture theater. Phase IV of the building followed approximately a year behind Phase III, overlapping with some construction activities of the previous phase. The completed project now provides Orange County with a world-class facility for a variety of trade shows and conventions, to cater to an ever-increasing meetings market.

The Phase III expansion organized common-use specialty spaces, such as the ballroom, auditorium, and food service areas around a 70-foot atrium space accessed through the primary entrance to the complex. A sweeping, inverted ceiling vault was designed to capture and reflect natural light pouring into the space from large clerestories on each side. The main entrance, leading into the atrium lobby, is a full-height wall of glass that blurs the boundary between interior and exterior space. The scale of the entrance and atrium space dominates the building's façade. Its soaring height and curved form represent open arms, welcoming visitors into the building.

TVS was committed to continuing the styles established during the earlier Phase II expansion in their designs for Phase III in order to unify the look of the entire facility. The architecture for the expansion made use of existing materials, finishes, and previously used detailing. The architects created dramatic new volumes at strategic locations to provide spatial variety and to aid in orientation throughout this large facility.

The dominant use of precast concrete on the building's façade helps to extend the character of the existing structures. The TVS team used precast concrete extensively in the building's concourses and lobbies to provide a smooth architectural transition from exterior to interior. Within the building, the patterns of both the terrazzo and carpet take their inspiration from the Orlando area's lush foliage. The building's color palette is composed of soft pastels in keeping with the Central Florida theme.

Neon lighting rims the edge of the structure on all phases, visually tying them into one complex.

Sweeping inverted ceiling vaults capture light and suggest movement through the main entrance.

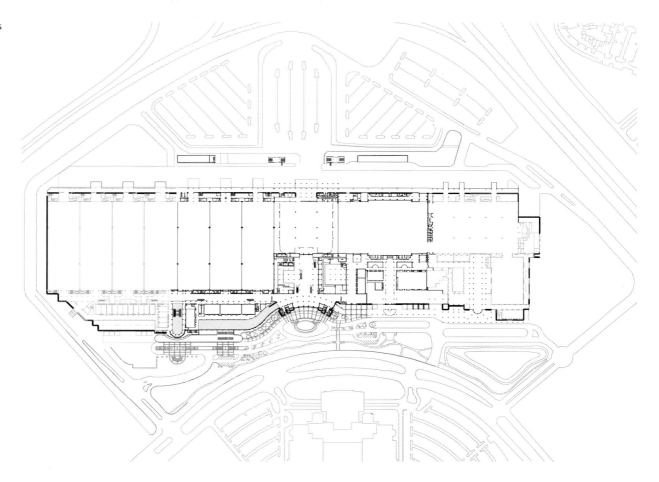

Orange County site plan, Phases I-IV

Dramatic entrances will welcome convention attendees to a new 2.5-million-square-foot exhibit hall when Phase V is completed.

Carpeting and the vaulted ceiling direct movement through the main entrance lobby.

One of the three entrances brings guests into a 3-level atrium surrounded by meeting rooms, before leading them to the expansive 1.5-million-square-foot exhibit hall.

The main entrance overlooks a
five-acre public plaza and
crescent-shaped fountain.

McCormick Place Convention Center

Chicago, Illinois 1996

TVS won a competition sponsored by the Metropolitan Pier and Exposition Authority (MPEA) to design the 2.5 million-square-foot expansion of McCormick Place, Chicago's premier convention and civic center. The completed expansion distinguishes the complex as the world's largest convention and trade show facility with over 2.1 million square feet of exhibition space. The McCormick Place South Building, the facility's second major expansion since 1971, augmented the facility's ability to accommodate increasingly larger trade shows and conventions. While the main goal of the expansion was the provision of additional exhibition space, the increased meeting space was intended to accommodate conventions, a greater economic asset to the city. The architects met with various government agencies, commissions, public forums, and neighborhood and special interest groups to define the program and review concepts. The design process included major presentations by the architects to the governor, the mayor, and their staffs to gain direct input, approval, and support.

The architects faced the challenges of creating a major entrance of appropriate scale for Chicago's convention center and trade complex, connecting all three buildings with a public concourse, and maximizing the flexibility of the exhibition hall floor space. The addition of a 900,000-square-foot exhibition hall was connected at the same level with McCormick Place's existing North Halls and to the East Halls with an extension of the concourse. Further additions include 134,000 square feet of meeting space and a 34,000-square-foot ballroom.

The city wanted to establish an "economic engine" in an under-utilized area in order to enhance future development and property value. This mandate generated several urban design issues and prompted the architects to propose several large-scale moves. The first called for the elimination of vehicular traffic through the center of the existing complex which separated the exhibit buildings. TVS substituted new connections from the complex to commuter rail and transportation systems serving as a link between the neighborhood to the west of the development and Lake Michigan, and clear, recognizable, pedestrian connections between existing and new developments. Finally, the design team introduced in front of the new entrance a five-acre public space, which is both commensurate with the scale of the complex and an inviting environment for the general public. The space is defined by the new entrance and exhibit halls, the 800-room McCormick Place Hyatt Regency Hotel, also designed by TVS, and five 75-foot tall light pylons. A great crescent-shaped water feature bordering a large lawn is the focal point of the space.

The expansion's success created additional program needs. As a result, the MPEA commissioned TVS to design McCormick Place a new 3,500-car parking structure, new office space, and additional conference facilities.

The structure borders the public square on the west with conference facilities which overlook the square and forming the fourth side of a great urban room. The central architectural element in the expansion is the 1,360 foot-long, 110 foot-high concourse, which links the exhibition halls of all three phases of the complex, and redefines the center of the complex. The Grand Concourse extends from the main entrance at the public square on the west end and continues as a pedestrian bridge crossing over Lake Shore Drive to the East Building and the lake beyond.

Sculptural Venetian plastered walls and more than 100 fountains animate the space and punctuate directional changes to meeting functions. An east concourse serves meeting rooms that overlook the lake. A west concourse serves other meeting rooms and the ballroom. The architects located the ballroom adjacent to the main entrance so that it would be easily accessible for local events without forcing attendees to move through the entire facility.

McCormick Place is a highly visible landmark in this area just south of Chicago's downtown loop. The TVS design continues the architectural vocabulary of museums and cultural institutions that run along the southern section of the lakeshore and has become a catalyst for redevelopment in the area. The new plaza, now known as McCormick Square, has proven to be popular with convention goers and residents from surrounding neighborhoods. TVS was awarded the 2001 AIA National Honor Award for the design of this Chicago landmark.

The exterior architecture combines substantial columns with a lighter grid of glass wall fenestration.

Meeting Room level

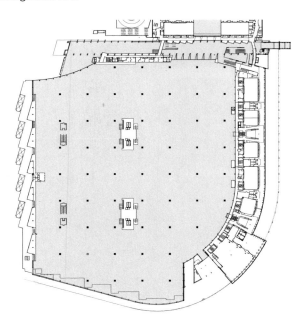

Exhibit Hall level

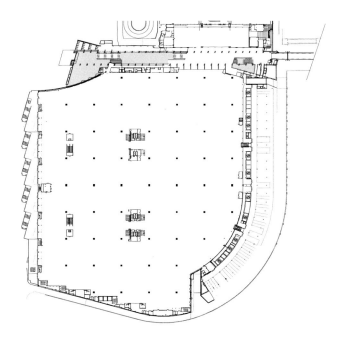

Ground level

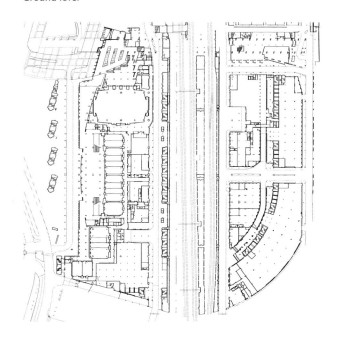

Dramatic light pylons announce the arrival court and grand plaza to arriving guests.

Loading docks are discreetly tucked beneath circulation areas to minimize visibility.

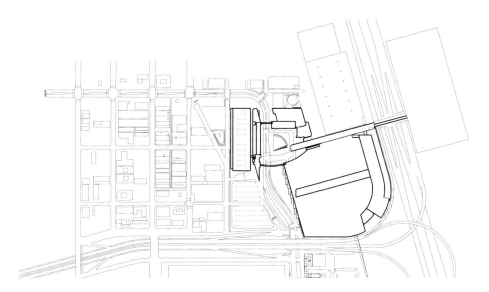

McCormick Place site plan

The pedestrian bridge, highlighted by massive light pylons, extends the grand concourse to the East Building and the lake shore beyond.

The concourse stair and escalator create a processional approach from the lobby to the upper levels.

The lobby assumes the overwhelming expanse, from the concourse to the glass façade of the main entrance.

Horizontal and vertical banding
in the architectural detailing
provides cohesive expression
throughout McCormick's
interior and exterior.

Water features animate
the interior circulation spaces.

143

McCormick Place Hyatt Regency Hotel

Chicago, Illinois 1998

Continuing in the spirit of the original expansion, TVS designed the 32-floor Hyatt Regency Hotel as part of the McCormick Place Convention Center development. The hotel is the tallest structure south of the Chicago Loop. Using geometric forms and dramatic rooftop lighting, the architects provided a visual landmark for the McCormick Place Convention Center.

The hotel provides a direct, enclosed link to the McCormick Place Grand Concourse for hotel guests and parking garage patrons. The architectural solution for the hotel clearly adapts and continues the design vocabulary established for the original convention center expansion. In their design of the hotel's roof, the architects provide a similar, dramatic, hovering mass without diminishing the impact of the Grand Concourse roof. Materials and textures on the hotel's exterior are similar to those used in the convention center. The two facilities complement each other architecturally and create an important public space at McCormick Place.

The design of this full-service hotel includes 800 guestrooms, including 48 specialty suites. Additional spaces include a 12,000-square-foot divisible ballroom, a 300-seat restaurant, a 250-seat bar, boardrooms, a business center, a health club with an indoor lap pool, and a retail shop.

The 32-floor structure, with its dramatic roofline, is a visual landmark for the McCormick Place Complex.

Glass paneling on the hotel's main façade mirrors the appearance of the hotel tower's fenestration.

The focal point for both the hotel and convention center is McCormick Plaza, with its crescent-shaped water feature.

Ground floor

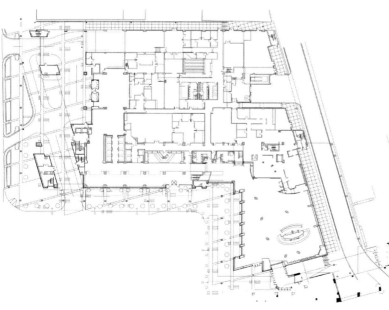

Second floor level

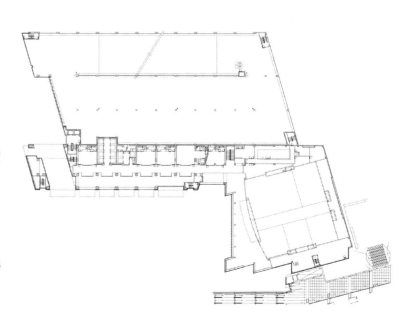

A covered loggia area at the hotel's exterior leads to the convention center and provides sun shading for the lobby.

Typical guest room

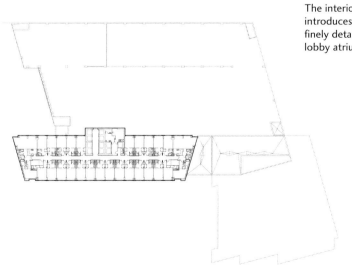

The interior design program introduces wood paneling and finely detailed flooring in the lobby atrium.

Interface Ray C. Anderson Plant

West Point, Georgia 1997

TVS was commissioned to design a plant and customer center that would express Interface C.E.O. Ray C. Anderson's corporate vision as well as the company's commitment to producing state-of-the-art products. The company's successful carpet tufting plant could no longer support the frequent customer tours and required renovation. The clients wanted to construct a new customer service center and warehouse manufacturing facility that would express their commitment to their employees, customers, and the environment. Throughout the project, the client's team, composed of executive and manufacturing administrative staff, met regularly to review the overall progress and goals of the project. The client's design objectives were informed by several goals: a renewed image, a new "flattened" hierarchy, and an interest in sustainable design practices.

The TVS team incorporated a new entrance for both employees and customers into the design for the new customer service center. The "science tower" serves as a focal point, straddling the expanded warehouse, the manufacturing facilities, and the existing plant. This structure symbolizes the technological and creative qualities of the products made by Interface. The floor is made of concrete raised access panels, made by Interface, which connect visually between the office and the plant.

The multimedia customer service center was designed to display the client's products while illustrating the company's commitment to sustainability. The architects created a highly flexible space that has been completed with a raw, unfinished quality. Glowing video monitors, displaying the company's product, are integrated into the design of a stone wall or "hearth," symbolizing the idea of a corporate family.

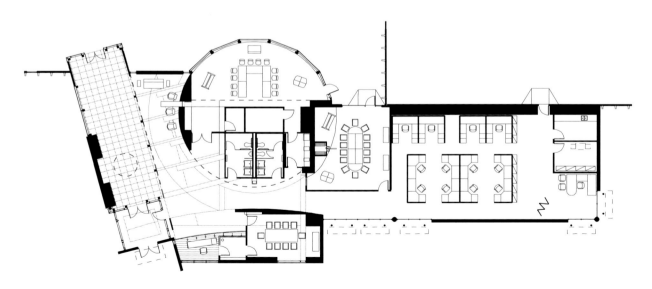

Floor plan, Customer Service Center

Metal grills are used as decorative accents throughout the facility; roof structures and overhang shading devices incorporate this textured material.

Natural stone and wood serve as a counterpoint to the glass and steel geometry of the curtainwall structure.

The glass wall and ocular skylight maximize natural light in the lobby. The stone wall features video display monitors.

Overhang shading devices diffuse light coming through the windows. Golden perforated grills, mounted on steel beams, are tilted downward.

The lobby educates visitors about the product. Movable stands exhibit an historical overview of the company, while overhead wall displays express the company's philosophy. These presentations are visible from the seating area.

A visual connection is established between the office facilities and the manufacturing plant.

Worcester
Convention Center

Worcester, Massachusetts 1997

TVS architects designed this new 190,000-square-foot convention center that is attached to an existing arena in a New England urban setting. The convention center is the gateway and focal point of Worcester's downtown area. Its progressive design enhances Worcester's image as a growing city. The architects expanded the existing 10,000-seat arena into a full-service civic, convention, and trade center, which includes a new 50,000-square-foot exhibition hall placed at the arena hall level.

The design solution for this large addition, located on a confined site, established a vertical organization of function spaces. A linear flanking concourse serves to activate a major downtown boulevard as it provides access to the convention center's spaces. This contemporary building was inspired by the rhythm and dignity of older civic buildings, providing a fitting link to the city's industrial heritage. Each façade incorporates major public entrances and sun-lit circulation zones. A strong dialogue exists between interior spaces and views of the major circulation arteries, which converge on the site.

The architects accommodated the tight, urban site by placing the 12,000-square-foot full-service ballroom and 17,500 square feet of additional meeting rooms above the exhibition hall. The multi-level design creates the necessary space by placing entrances and pre-function areas at primary access points.

Entrances are located at the convention center's primary access points, defined by the city's major transportation arteries.

The exterior façade incorporates extensive glazing to create a strong dialogue between interior spaces and the urban setting.

Administrative offices are fitted along the perimeter of the structure to provide staff with daylight and views.

The exterior custom designed light fixtures on the façade complement the architectural aesthetic.

Ribbed metal panels harmonize with custom concrete masonry units, adding a textural quality to the exterior and recalling the city's industrial heritage.

Within the concourse, escalators provide access to the three convention center levels.

Custom designed Axminster carpet brings an element of vitality to the convention center's interior.

Ground floor plan

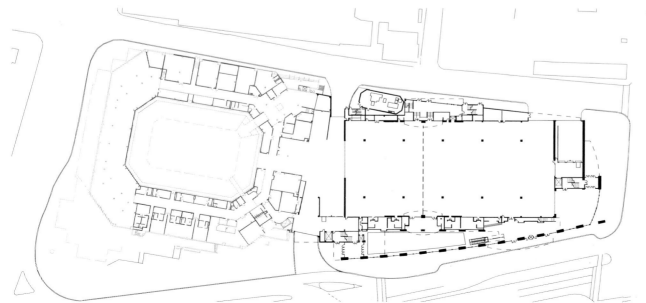

Plaza Vespucio and Plaza Tobalaba

Santiago, Chile 1998

TVS has designed several projects in South America, which reinforce the importance of public spaces within commercial projects. Encouraged by clients who are setting out to build their developments as new town centers, TVS has incorporated large outdoor plazas, amphitheaters, public parks, outdoor café seating areas, and children's play areas in their designs. Projects such as the expansion of Plaza Vespucio's entertainment center and the construction of Plaza Tobalaba, both located in Santiago, Chile, reflect this public attitude.

Plaza Vespucio, located in Santiago's prosperous La Florida district, was originally constructed as a single level dumbbell-shaped mall. TVS completely transformed and vertically expanded the center to respond to La Florida's increasingly fashion-conscious shoppers. Like Plaza Tobalaba, Plaza Vespucio is now an active town center. Restaurants and cafés line the sidewalks, linking the food court with the newly-created rapid transit stop. Future development phases will tie professional office buildings and hotel towers to the center.

In conjunction with the vertical expansion, which doubled the amount of the leasable space, TVS transformed the mall's image. The dark interior became a dramatic new light-filled space.

The addition of the second level at Plaza Vespucio provided the opportunity to transform the dark interior into a dramatic, light-filled space.

By night, the drama provided by sun and shadow is replaced by the warm glow of the vaulted ceiling.

Ornamental trusswork supports the vaulted skylit roof, creating a grand, open, unifying space. A palette of neutral colors and patterned marble floors provide the interior with a level of sophistication that compliments Plaza Vespucio's new fashionable image.

TVS designers master planned Plaza Tobalaba to capture views of the mountain range that runs along the southeastern edge of Santiago. The building's plan is crescent-shaped, embracing an open air plaza that serves both as a community park and an arrival court for the center. Through this configuration, TVS achieved the client's goal of creating a community center with opportunities for entertainment and social interaction. Plaza Tobalaba's entertainment venues, including a cinema and an arcade, sculpt the building's façade. In the evening, these venues are highlighted as the center becomes a beacon of light. The vaulted roof and transparent exterior skin of the food court, which are framed by the dramatic light towers, give the mall its dramatic image and strong visual axis from the street. This axis is reinforced by a series of plazas, and will be continued in future expansions.

The domed, elliptical center court of Plaza Tobalaba punctuates the midpoint of the retail concourse and forms the interior arrival court for the exterior entertainment plaza.

Open stairways cascade down from the outdoor dining balcony, connecting the Food Court with the activity of the open-air plaza.

At night, the food court is transformed into a colorful beacon of light for both the interior and exterior of the mall.

Merrill Lynch,
Jacksonville Operations Buildings

Jacksonville, Florida 1998

TVS designed an economical operations campus for Merrill Lynch. The goal was to create a campus of office buildings for the client's back-of-house operations that expressed a casual and friendly sense of community. The architects composed the complex so that individual buildings could be easily leased or sold, should the company require less space in the future.

The site selected for the Jacksonville Operations Building was an abandoned titanium mine, which provided a landscape generally devoid of vegetation and a gently rolling topography uncharacteristic of the locale. The mining operation had left a bog in the middle of the property. In response to these existing conditions, the TVS team designed a 27-acre lake as the centerpiece of a 130-acre plan for 11 office buildings. During Phases One and Two of the project, five buildings were constructed with approximately 700,000 square feet of space.

The architects responded to regional influences and created a friendly scale for the complex, which also met the needs of a modest budget. The design used a large, overhung, standing-seam metal roof to respond to a climate of intense sunshine and frequent downpours. The roof also created a striking image for Merrill Lynch. The articulated rose-colored concrete masonry skin gives the complex an inviting scale and a facility rich in detail. These structures are interconnected and clustered around the lake, yielding on intimate yet dramatic campus atmosphere.

The textured rose-colored concrete masonry gives the complex a rich and distinctive quality that is inviting to the tenants.

Site plan

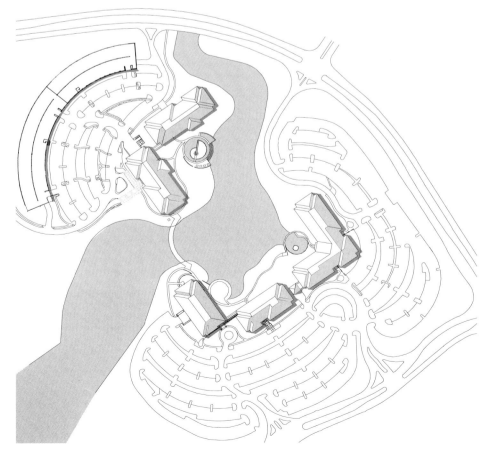

The building's overhanging, standing seam, metal roof responds to environmental concerns and creates a striking design feature.

Merrill Lynch,
Denver Operations Buildings

Denver, Colorado 1999

In their design of Merrill Lynch's Denver operations facility, TVS architects were concerned with creating a viable office-campus for their clients and an efficient, enjoyable environment for the employees. The team provided Merrill Lynch with a distinct architectural image well suited to its High Plains location. The total site program includes 1,000,000 square feet of office space in five buildings and parking for 5,000 cars on 70 acres of land in suburban Denver.

The architects conceived of the structure as a strong geometric shape in the expansive rolling plains. The parking structures and office buildings were organized to create an enclosure in the vast landscape, defining the campus and giving the employees a sense of place. The office buildings are positioned on the landscape to provide an impressive image when viewed from afar and provide the employees with a view of the front range of the Rocky Mountains.

The buildings are designed to harmonize with the site; they are strung together to form an exaggerated horizontal mass that addresses the immense scale of the prairie. The TVS team used stone plinths to root the buildings in the landscape. These plinths provide a horizontal datum on which to fix the buildings visually and create images of great stone jetties anchored in a sea of prairie grass.

Colorado rose sandstone is used throughout the campus, along with warm limestone-colored, pre-cast concrete. By using these materials, the architects relate the structure to its natural environment and provide a rugged architectural image. The design addresses the intensity of the Colorado sun and creates dramatic shadows across the building by using exposed structural steel members as a trellis and shading devices. The buildings have been designed as efficient rectangular masses, which provide flexible space.

For Building One, the TVS team divided the structure with a full-height atrium, which would be the heart of the campus. The cafeteria, training rooms, human resources, financial services, and other public services are accessed from within the atrium. The four-level space has three distinct zones, starting with the reception lobby in the east, traversing a linear indoor-garden in the middle, and culminating in a grand, landscaped interior space facing the mountain range to the west.

Building Two features a modest but sophisticated lobby. Here the architects designed a three-level art glass wall as a centerpiece for the simple cubic space. The glass elevators travel behind the transparent wall, providing visitors with a kinetic experience and a beautiful view of Pike's Peak as they travel to the fourth-floor presentation room.

Site plan

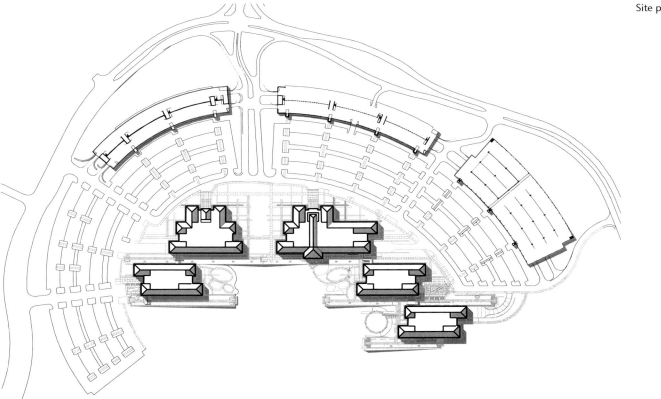

Colorado rose sandstone and
warm limestone-colored pre-
cast concrete relates the
building to its rugged, warm
surroundings.

The atrium's design creates the illusion of an open-air space below the gabled roof. Interior landscaping blurs the boundary between interior and exterior spaces.

Landscaping within the atrium incorporates a naturalistic running stream, with rocks and temperate plants. The illusory effect of the glass wall and ceiling is most evident when combined with brick grid walls that wrap around the corners of the space and form a gate to the exterior landscape.

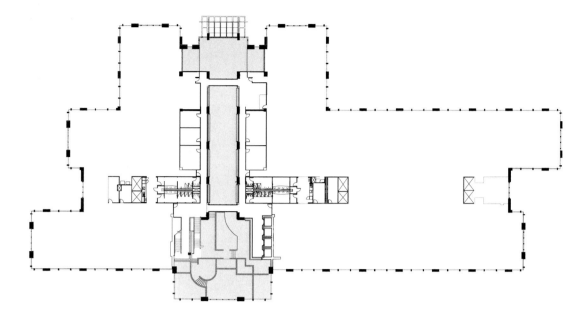

Typical floor plan

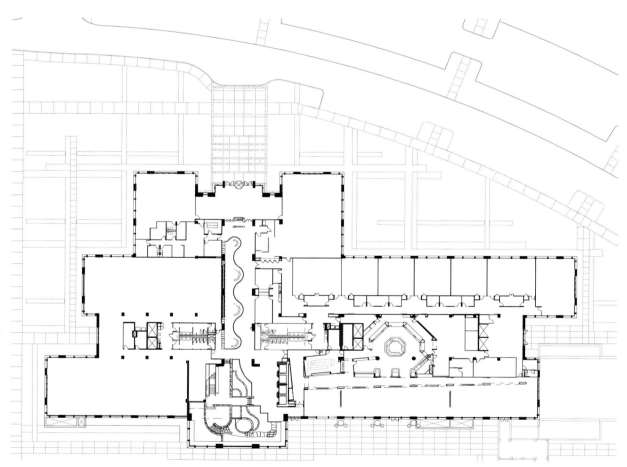

Lobby floor plan

Merrill Lynch,
Hopewell, New Jersey Campus

Hopewell, New Jersey 2002

The TVS design of the Merrill Lynch campus in Hopewell, New Jersey, allowed them to consolidate leased office properties totaling 800,000 square feet, which had been scattered throughout the Princeton, New Jersey area, into a single corporate campus. Office and amenity spaces constructed in the initial phase total approximately two million square feet. The project was master-planned to allow for continued incremental growth and to provide flexibility to react to external economic forces.

In response to the client's vision, TVS designed a meaningful campus environment that reinforces the concept of unity for the employees, while serving as a significant corporate symbol for the company. The campus is organized around a signature drive that is flanked by a series of three outdoor spaces. At the western entrance to the campus a nature park is organized around two ponds connected by a rocky brook. Progressing eastward, town center is a highly active space and the central focus of the campus. Town center is flanked by many of the campus amenities, including human resources, the post office, drycleaners, a medical suite and the main dining hall. Beyond this highly active space is the quiet, more formal, academic quadrangle.

By organizing the campus around these outdoor spaces, the architects established a sense of community among a variety of office and amenity buildings. The campus includes eight office buildings, four assembly/food service buildings, a health club, and structured parking. Covered arcades that connect the buildings at grade further strengthen the relationships between these various parts. Similarly organized below grade, a system of loading docks and service tunnels also connect each structure.

In addition to Merrill Lynch's interest in creating a pleasant and productive environment for their employees, goals included a practical sustainable design approach. TVS took special care to preserve all existing wetland and woodland areas. A commitment was made to utilize a combination of structured and surface parking to increase the permeable surface area of the development. Retention basins filter run-off before it is introduced into stream basins. Mechanical systems were centralized to maximize efficiency. Ice storage systems were designed to reduce peak demand energy use. Dual fuel systems were utilized for heating to insure that cost effective energy is available. Controlled outdoor lighting systems were designed to minimize light pollution and preserve the rural night sky.

At the culmination of the main entrance drive, guests are welcomed to the Merrill Lynch offices through the glazed lobby atrium.

The contemporary campus recalls the collegiate gothic architecture of numerous colleges and universities. The articulated brick and pre-cast façade lend a sense of tradition and sophistication to the corporate campus buildings.

The master plan is carefully organized to preserve wetlands while providing a distinctive campus environment with an academic quadrangle, a town center, and a natural park.

The manmade lake is the focal point of the park-like setting.

Hot Springs Convention Center

Hot Springs, Arkansas 1998

The Hot Springs Convention Center, the only convention facility located in a national park, creates a striking gateway to the Historic District and the Bath House Row of Hot Springs, Arkansas. The TVS design for the expanded convention center transformed the existing 70,000-square-foot civic center with an additional 75,000 square feet of exhibit space and 20,000 square feet of meeting space, as well as a new grand hall. The existing building was renovated to include a new 17,000-square-foot ballroom. This large-scale expansion was designed to meet the facility's operational and spatial needs, while sensitively responding to the small-scale architecture of the Historic District.

The existing civic center was a unique 1950's assembly hall with a stepped octagonal Bermuda roof. The well-known regional assembly hall was historically significant to the community. TVS's design updated the facility, while preserving the identity of the original structure. The exterior renovation incorporated forms and materials that unify the whole convention center.

Outdoor public spaces and pedestrian linkages through the building to the adjacent hotel, public park, and adjoining neighborhood and visitors' chapel enliven the streetscape. The public spaces are enhanced through bringing natural light into the concourse and lobby. The concourse serves as a museum, which houses a large permanent and rotating art collection.

The design of the convention center acknowledges its location adjacent to the Historic District, it breaks down the large scale of the building program to reflect the scale of the city. The architects incorporated details and materials reflective of the historic Bath House Row, which is the focus of the city and the national park. The center's entrance canopy and tower respond to familiar forms in the Hot Springs architectural environment.

The interior of the convention center incorporates an exposed wood ceiling and natural-colored, exposed wood roof structure, as well as yellow brick, stucco and limestone, all of which reflect the distinct materials found in the bathhouses. The detail of the custom carpet, with its aqueous forms, underscores the significance of the hot springs to the park and the community.

The expansion is successfully integrated into the Historic District through the bold use of familiar forms and materials. The carefully articulated and open façade creates a welcoming center.

Plan

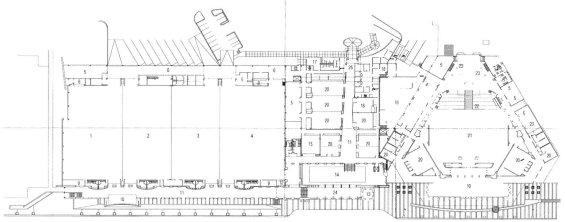

Natural light enters the
concourse and lobby through
extensive glazing and the
continuous clerestory.

The warmth and articulation of the exterior materials of limestone, brick, and wood respond sensitively to the smaller scale architecture of the Historic District.

The dramatically lit tower signals the entrance to the main lobby of the center.

The concourse is an appropriate setting for the permanent and revolving art collection housed in the center.

The interior incorporates natural materials of brick and wood, creating a warm and welcoming space for guests.

Mall of Georgia

Atlanta, Georgia 1999

TVS has consistently completed projects that acknowledge the capacity of retail spaces to serve as community centers. In metropolitan Atlanta, Mall of Georgia is the center of a new district known as Mill Creek. This district has residential components and a commercial core of several million square feet. The design of the 1.4 million-square-foot enclosed mall simulates a walk through Georgia that extends from the coastal regions in the south to the mountains in the north. The 125,000-square-foot village includes a bandstand and public green for both professional and community activities. The village streets were designed by TVS to recall small towns in Georgia. The village and entertainment components of the Mall of Georgia are unified to create a pleasant, creative, educational experience that appeals to local residents and tourists alike.

The Village bandshell forms the backdrop for community-centered events. Visiting the mall and attending one of its many musical performances is a common experience for shoppers.

Children enjoy the interactive fountain in front of the main entrance to the Food Court. The façade recalls Atlanta's old Union Train Station.

The entertainment center is anchored by the I-Max and the cinema complex that ties directly to the Food Court, creating the social hub of the center.

The Food Court is designed to recall the historic nineteenth century Union Station train shed. Its focal point is a 15-foot diameter clock, which crowns the delightful top of the feature elevator tower.

A North Georgia Mountain Lodge feeling is conveyed by the interior design of the "Mountain Court".

The "Piedmont Wing" links the department stores together. Interiors and graphics reflect the Piedmont Region of Georgia.

Washington, D.C. Convention Center

Washington, D.C. 2003

When the TVS team took on the project of designing the Washington, D.C. Convention Center for the Washington Convention Center Authority, they also took on the responsibility of emphasizing the city's status as a nationally prominent meeting and convention destination. The architects had to reconcile several competing urban issues. The site is the culmination of a series of public monuments that begin at the Mall and continue north along Eighth Street to the convention center site on the north edge of Mount Vernon Square, spanning the blocks between Seventh and Ninth Streets. The square is home to the historic Carnegie Library, while the other surrounding blocks along L, M, and N Streets are residential. The challenge was to create a design formal, powerful, and appropriate for the nation's capital, but evocative of warmth and hospitality, while respecting the surrounding neighborhood architecture.

The solution is a building composed of three linked elements, which sit between Seventh and Ninth Streets. The main entrance to the convention center faces the square to the south. The architects mirrored the library's symmetrical design by centering the main lobby on axis with the library. The transparent ceremonial entrance to the lobby is flanked on either side by large masses of stone and pre-cast concrete, which mimic the color and texture of the library's limestone massing. As the complex stretches north, its height decreases and its skin turns to the familiar brick of the smaller surrounding commercial and residential structures to the east, west, and north sides.

Along with the urban issues, the architects faced programmatic challenges. Market studies indicated that the new convention center would need to provide 700,000 square feet of exhibit hall space and 210,000 square feet of meeting room space, including a 60,000-square-foot ballroom, in order to capture the city's target market in the meeting and convention industry. The facility also required approximately 1,390,000 square feet of space to accommodate circulation, food service, and administrative services. In the end, the program would demand a total gross area of 2,300,000 square feet. To compound the problem of accommodating such an enormous area within the allowed envelope, the architects had to adhere to the District's severe height restrictions on all construction. By placing two-thirds of the exhibit space below ground, the architects stayed within the height limitations and reduced the bulk of the building.

The architects designed all of the building's internal public-circulation elements, such as concourses, registration areas, and lobbies, around the perimeter of the building in order to access natural light. This treatment resulted in a transparent, active, friendly façade. The design situates meeting rooms in close proximity to exhibition halls for convenient movement between these two functions. A grand ballroom is located on the top level of the south block, overlooking Mount Vernon Square. The southern façade of the building is a large urban window that reaches from the street to the ballroom level. This design allows visitors a spectacular view of the city and its monuments from the ballroom's anteroom.

This new convention center will provide Washington, D.C. with a new landmark. The facility is efficient and marketable, yet sensitive and responsive to the adjacent neighborhoods. Now the nation's capital can claim prominence as a seat of commerce as well as the seat of government.

9th Street elevation

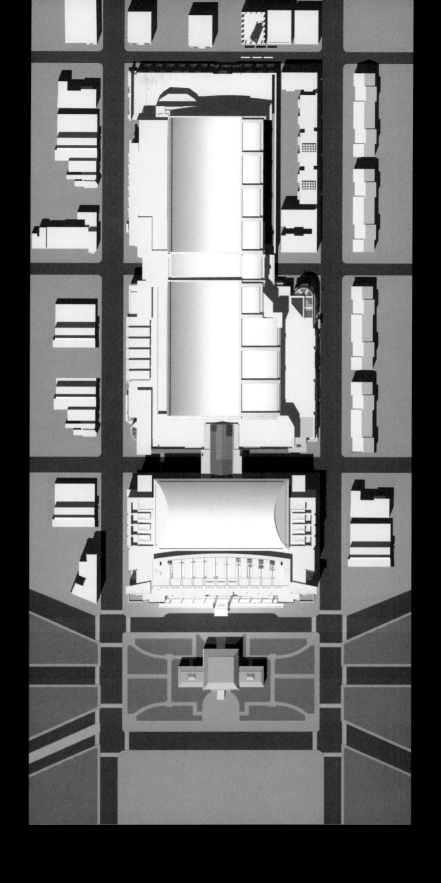

The site plan consists of three multi-block masses linked by spanning elements over the existing surface streets.

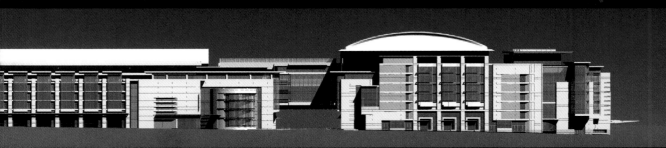

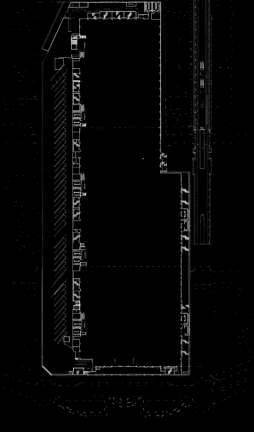

Level +36 Exhibit Hall

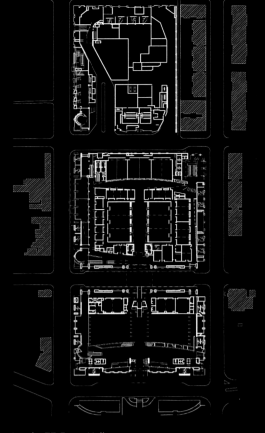

Level +77 Entry Hall

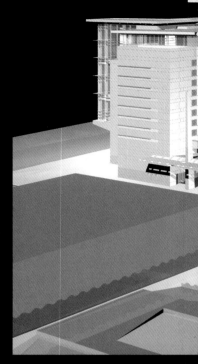

South Block,
 Mt. Vernon Street Entry

Level +111 Assembly Hall

Level 137 Grand Ballroom

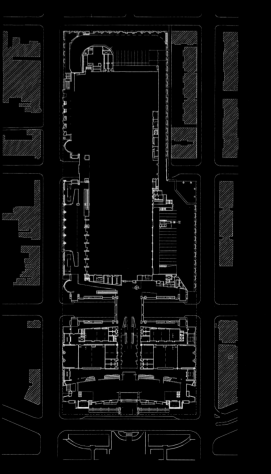

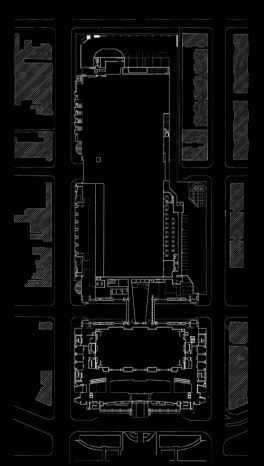

Longitudinal section

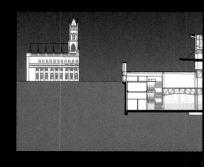

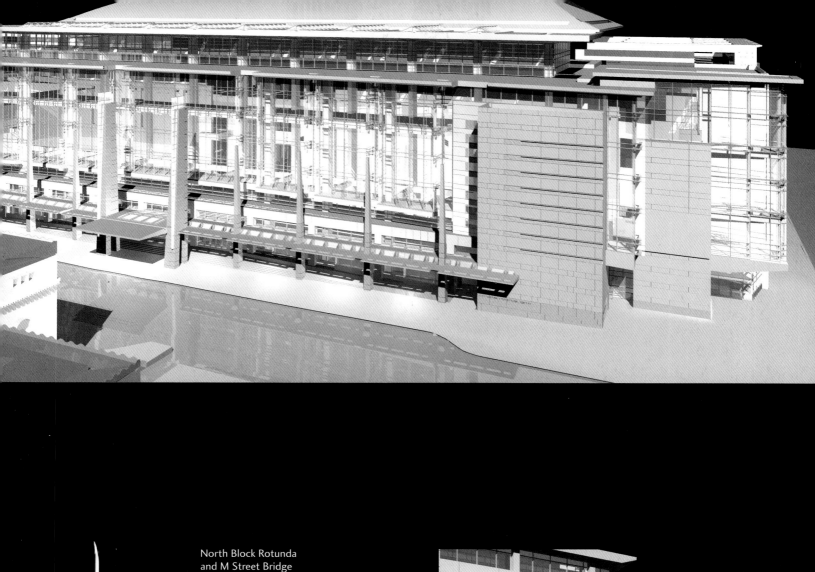

North Block Rotunda
and M Street Bridge

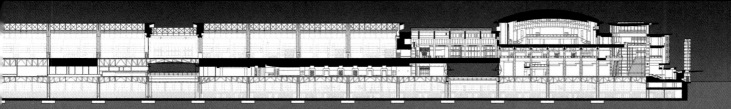

7th Street elevation

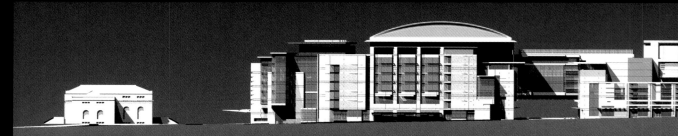

Monumental pylons recall
8th Street from Le Enfant's
city plan and identify the main
entry into the building.

The grand lobby is the primary
arrival space of the building.
The curving wood wall is visible
through the transparent south
elevation, becoming a final
layer to the exterior façade.

Credits

adidas International Southeast Regional Sales Office
ATLANTA, GEORGIA

Client
adidas America

Architecture/Interior Design
Smith Dalia Architects

TVS Interior Design Team
Libby Sims Patrick
Lucy Aiken-Johnson

Photographer
© Brian Gassel

Charlotte Convention Center
CHARLOTTE, NORTH CAROLINA

Client
City of Charlotte

TVS Design Team

DESIGN PRINCIPAL
Thomas W. Ventulett, III

STUDIO PRINCIPAL
C. Andrew McLean

PROJECT MANAGER
Jack Plaxco

PROJECT ARCHITECTS
Don Benz, Jay Thomson,
Ken Stockdell

PROJECT TEAM
Chuck Baxter,
Chris Curley, Tony Pickett

TVS Interior Design Team
Liz Neiswander,
Shannon Dixon,
Laura Ferreira,
Candace FitzGerald,
Holley Henderson

Associate Architect
The FWA Group

Photographer
© Brian Gassel

Concourse Complex and Towers
ATLANTA, GEORGIA

Client
The Landmarks Group
(Buildings I, II, IV, V, VI)

TVS Design Team

PRINCIPAL OF RECORD
Raymond F. Stainback, Jr.

STUDIO PRINCIPAL
Ray C. Hoover III

PROJECT MANAGERS
Jerry Stephenson,
Bill Murry,
Gene Montezinos

PROJECT ARCHITECTS
Karen Choate,
Thom O'Brien
Howard Baker

PROJECT TEAM
Behr Champana,
Teresa Edmisten,
William Edmisten,
Nicholas Wolfcale,
Nancy Cartledge
Gary Flesher
Kirstin Eriksson
Rebekah Wang

Associate Architect
Brown Design Associates
(Building IV)

Photographers
© Brian Gassel
© E. Alan McGee

Doubletree Hotel at Concourse
ATLANTA, GEORGIA

Client
The Landmarks Group

TVS Design Team

PRINCIPAL OF RECORD
Raymond F. Stainback, Jr.

PROJECT ARCHITECT
Jere Williams

PROJECT MANAGER
Gene Montezinos

PROJECT TEAM
Teresa Edmisten, William
Edmisten, Robert Meaders

Associate Architect
Millkey & Brown

Photographers
© Brian Gassel
© E. Alan McGee

Georgia Dome
ATLANTA, GEORGIA

Client
Georgia World Congress
Center Authority

TVS Design Team

DESIGN PRINCIPAL
Thomas W. Ventulett, III

PRINCIPAL OF RECORD
Raymond F. Stainback, Jr.

STUDIO PRINCIPAL
Philip A. Junger

PROJECT TEAM
Paul Degenkolb,
William Edmisten,
Gary Fowler,
Jerry Stephenson

TVS Interior Design
Paula Stafford

Joint Venture Architects
Heery International
Rosser International, Inc.

Associate Architect
Allain & Associates, Inc.

Photographers
© Brian Gassel
© Timothy Hursley

Georgia International Plaza
ATLANTA, GEORGIA

Client
State of Georgia / Georgia
World Congress Center
Authority

TVS Design Team

DESIGN PRINCIPAL
Thomas W. Ventulett, III

STUDIO PRINCIPAL
C. Andrew McLean

PROJECT MANAGER
Ed Stripling

PROJECT ARCHITECT
Jay Thomson

PROJECT TEAM
Ken Stockdell,
Leslee Hare James,
Henri Tchaya

Associate Architect
Allain & Associates, Inc.

Photographer
© Brian Gassel

Georgia World Congress Center (Phases I, II, III, V)
ATLANTA, GEORGIA

Client
Georgia World Congress
Center Authority

(Phase I) TVS Design Team

DESIGN PRINCIPAL
Thomas W. Ventulett, III

PRINCIPAL OF RECORD
Raymond F. Stainback, Jr.

PROJECT MANAGER
Byron Chapman

PROJECT ARCHITECTS
Michael H. Ezell,
Andrew McLean,
Helen Hatch, John Wyle

PROJECT TEAM
Bob Colyer, Gary Cornell,
Joseph Molloy, Jim Ward

(Phase II) TVS Design Team

DESIGN PRINCIPAL
Thomas W. Ventulett, III

PRINCIPAL OF RECORD
Raymond F. Stainback, Jr.

PROJECT MANAGER
C. Andrew McLean

PROJECT ARCHITECTS
Gary Fowler, Jack Plaxco,
Ed Stripling, Jim Ward

PROJECT TEAM
Behr Champana,
Brad Ellis, Mike Ezell,
Steve Johnson,
Andy McNeilly,
Richard McCann,
Gar Muse, Liz Neiswander,
Wayne Shoemake,
Audrey S Standifer,
Ken Stockdell,
Jim Woodcox

TVS Interior Design
Margo Jones, Laurie Born,
Carol Higgins,
Paula Stafford

Photographer
© Brian Gassel

(Phase III) TVS Design Team

DESIGN PRINCIPAL
Thomas W. Ventulett, III

PRINCIPAL OF RECORD
Raymond F. Stainback, Jr.

STUDIO PRINCIPAL
C. Andrew McLean

PROJECT TEAM
Ed Stripling, Jay Thomson,
Alex Zaretsky

TVS interior design team
Liz Neiswander,
Shannon Dixon, Julie Prinz

Photographer
© Brian Gassel

(Phase IV) TVS Design Team

DESIGN PRINCIPAL
Thomas W. Ventulett, III

STUDIO PRINCIPAL
C. Andrew McLean

PROJECT MANAGER
Jay Thomson

PROJECT ARCHITECTS
John Stephenson,
Ed Stripling

PROJECT TEAM
Laura Ahern,
Robert Alden, John Cantù,
Howard Chen,
Hal Doughty, Marvin Flax,
Wright Gardner, Aaron
Gentry, Anna Gillon,
Ana Maria Leon, Bill
Martin, James Riley,
Mishael Lake,
Allen Stewart

TVS Interior Design Team
Liz Neiswander,
Jennifer Davis Bricken,
Holley Henderson,
Phillip Jeffries

Photographer
© Brian Gassel

Hot Springs Convention Center
HOT SPRINGS, ARKANSAS

Client
City of Hot Springs

TVS Design Team

SENIOR PRINCIPAL
Michael H. Ezell

PROJECT MANAGER
Ken Stockdell

PROJECT ARCHITECTS
Jay Thomson,
Rob Svedberg

TVS Interior Design Team
Candace FitzGerald,
Holley Henderson,
Anna Lisa Brown

Associate Architects
Wittenberg,
Delony & Davidson, Inc.,
The Wilcox Group, Arnold
& Associates

Photographer
© Brian Gassel

Interface Ray C. Anderson Plant
WEST POINT, GEORGIA

Client
Interface Flooring Systems

TVS Design Team

SENIOR PRINCIPAL
Ray C. Hoover, III

STUDIO PRINCIPAL
William R. Halter

PROJECT TEAM
Glenn Grosse, Tonja Adair,
Ed Palisoc

TVS Interior Design Team
Michele Lyden,
Jennifer Davis Bricken

Photographer
© Brian Gassel

King of Prussia
KING OF PRUSSIA, PENNSYLVANIA

Clients
Kravco Company
The Yarmouth Group

TVS Design Team

SENIOR PRINCIPAL
Thomas Porter

STUDIO PRINCIPAL
Mark Carter

PROJECT TEAM
Bill Abballe, Chuck
Baxter, Stephan Carlin,
Rick Casey, Dots Colley,
Ross Davis, Allen Dedels,
Lee Ann Gamble,
Mercedes Laudano,
Thom O'Brien,
Eric Wilson, Tony Pickett,
Diego Aguayo, Alex Kirk,
Bill Halter, Gary Flesher

TVS Interior Design Team
Donna Childs,
Deborah Lee,
Michele Lyden

Photographer
© Brian Gassel

Long Beach Convention Center
LONG BEACH, CALIFORNIA

Client
City of Long Beach

TVS Design Team

SENIOR PRINCIPAL
H. Preston Crum

ARCHITECT OF RECORD
Robert N. Veale

PROJECT MANAGER
Foster Lynn

PROJECT ARCHITECT
Maria Bonau-Barker

PROJECT TEAM
William Edmisten,
Anna Gillon,
Paul Monardo,
Eric Richardson

TVS Interior Design Team
Paula Stafford,
Stephanie Belcher

Photographer
© Brian Gassel

Mall of Georgia at Mill Creek
GWINNETT COUNTY, GEORGIA

Client
Mall of Georgia,
LLC Simon Property
Group, Ben Carter
Properties

TVS Design Team

SENIOR PRINCIPAL
Thomas Porter

PROJECT MANAGER
Butch Birchfield

PROJECT ARCHITECTS
Glenn Bethel,
Joseph Molloy,
Jeff Wierenga

PROJECT TEAM
Denise Chiafolo,
Akash Guar, Ted Hitch,
Florence Hosein,

Rob Mercer, Joe Minatta,
Ryan Miller,
Richard Rounds,
Derrick Rowe,
Henri Tchaya ,
Kenneth Whitted

TVS Interior Design Team
Donna Childs,
Michele Lyden,
Jessica Marro, Susan
Watts, Jennifer Davis
Bricken, Zoë Rawlins,
Leslie Spievack

Photographer:
© Brian Gassel

McCormick Place Convention Center
CHICAGO, ILLINOIS

Client
Metropolitan Pier &
Exposition Authority

TVS Design Team

DESIGN PRINCIPAL
Thomas W. Ventulett III

STUDIO PRINCIPAL
C. Andrew McLean

PROJECT MANAGER
Paul Duckwall

PROJECT ARCHITECTS
Philip Junger,
Scott Sickeler,
Ken Stockdell,
Nicholas Wolfcale

PROJECT TEAM
Robert Fischel,
Peter Green, Scot Macrae,
Baker Mallory, Bill Renz,
Eddie Rhinehart,
Julie Sanford, Mark Scialo,
Jim Simmons,
Jay Thomson, Ron Ward,
Kathy Wilson,
Brad Winkeljohn

TVS Interior Design Team
Liz Neiswander,
Shannon Dixon,
Laura Ferreira,
Holley Henderson

Design Builder
Mc3D Inc. (a design /
construction consortium)
The Clark Construction
Group
Huber, Hunt & Nichols
Inc.
Morse Diesel International
Inc.
Walsh Construction
Company of Illinois
Louis Jones Enterprises
Inc.
Alex Munoz General
Contractor
Mesirow Stein Real Estate
A. Epstein & Sons
International, Inc.§

Consulting Architects
D'Escoto, Inc.
Ross Barney & Jankowski,
Inc.

Photographer
© Brian Gassel

Hyatt Regency McCormick Place
CHICAGO, ILLINOIS

Client
Metropolitan Pier &
Exposition Authority

TVS Design Team

SENIOR PRINCIPAL
Thomas W. Ventulett III

STUDIO PRINCIPAL
Philip A. Junger

PROJECT MANAGER
Maria Bonau-Barker

PROJECT TEAM
Dennis Carr, J.P. Hwang,
Tom Ingram, Sangjin Lee,
Scot Macrae, Micah Rosen,
Jerry Stephenson

Associate Architect
A. Epstein and Sons
International, Inc.

Photographer
© Brian Gassel

Merrill Lynch, Denver Operations Building
DENVER, COLORADO

Client
Merrill Lynch & Company,
Inc.

TVS Design Team

SENIOR PRINCIPAL
Michael H. Ezell

STUDIO PRINCIPAL
Gary Fowler

PROJECT MANAGER
Carleen Waller

PROJECT TEAM
Teresa Edmisten,
Robert Svedberg

TVS Interior Design
Nancy Cartledge,
Daunn Guthrie,
Jason Bailey, D.J. Betsill,
Rena Howard,
Michele McConnell,
Nancy Westbrook,
Wanda Wenger

Photographer
© Brian Gassel

Merrill Lynch, Hopewell, New Jersey Campus
HOPEWELL, NEW JERSEY

Client
Merrill Lynch & Company,
Inc.

TVS Design Team

SENIOR PRINCIPAL
Michael H. Ezell

STUDIO PRINCIPAL
Gary Fowler

PROJECT MANAGER
William Edmisten

PROJECT ARCHITECT
Robert Svedberg

PROJECT TEAM
Ed Alshut, Jason Bailey,
Robert Bielamowicz,
Sandra Davis, Brian Egan,
Mike Estes, Jeff Powell,
Joe Remling,
Susan Shepard,
Whitney Shephard,

Jennifer Turpin, Wanda
Wenger, Gina Rickett,
James Riley, J.P. Hwang,
Dave Brown

TVS Interior Design Team

STUDIO PRINCIPAL
Steven W. Clem

PROJECT TEAM
Mac Hicks, Phillip Jeffries,
Taylor Robinson,
Shawn Alshut

Renderings
Dan Harmon

Merrill Lynch, Jacksonville Operations Building
JACKSONVILLE, FLORIDA

Client
Merrill Lynch & Company,
Inc.

TVS Design Team

SENIOR PRINCIPAL
Michael H. Ezell

STUDIO PRINCIPAL
Gary Fowler

PROJECT ARCHITECTS
Don Benz,
Teresa Edmisten,
Nicholas Wolfcale

PROJECT TEAM
Dan Berman, Rick Elliott,
Jeff Phillips,
Eddie Rhinehart,
Carleen Waller, Ron Ward,
Nancy Westbrooks

TVS Interior Design Team
Mac Hicks, Ben Magee,
Joan Moore-Moone,
Jason Bailey

Photographer
© Brian Gassel

Mobile Convention Center
MOBILE, ALABAMA

Client
City of Mobile

TVS Design Team

DESIGN PRINCIPAL
Thomas W. Ventulett, III

PRINCIPAL OF RECORD
Raymond F. Stainback, Jr.

STUDIO PRINCIPAL
C. Andrew McLean

DESIGN TEAM
Don Benz, David Hubbard,
Ken Stockdell

TVS Interior Design Team
Liz Neiswander,
Shannon Dixon,
Julie Prinz, Barri Studeras

Associate Architect
The Architects Group, Inc.

Consulting Architect
David Jones Jr. &
Associates, Inc.

Photographer
© Brian Gassel

Orange County Convention Center (Phase III)
ORLANDO, FLORIDA

Client
Orange County

TVS Design Team

STUDIO PRINCIPAL
C. Andrew McLean

PROJECT MANAGER
Jim Ward

PROJECT ARCHITECT
Jim Mehserle

PROJECT TEAM
Yann Cowart,
Leslee Hare James,
Alex Zaretsky

TVS Interior Design Team
Interior Design Concepts,
Inc., Jacksonville, Florida

Associate Architect
Hunton, Brady, Pryor, Maso
Architects, Orlando, Florida

Consulting Architects
Gonzalez Heindrick Design
C.T. Shu
Helen Davis Hatch
Architects, Inc.

Photographer
© Brian Gassel

Pennsylvania Convention Center
PHILADELPHIA, PENNSYLVANIA

Client
Pennsylvania Convention
Center Authority

TVS Design Team

DESIGN PRINCIPAL
Thomas W. Ventulett , III

STUDIO PRINCIPAL
C. Andrew McLean

PROJECT MANAGER
Kenneth J. Bryson

PROJECT TEAM
Behr Champana,
Gary Fowler, Kim Martin,
Randy Maxwell, Jack Plaxco,
Ken Stockdell, Jim Ward

TVS Interior Design Team
Liz Neiswander,
Paula Stafford,
Shannon Dixon

*Associate Architect /
Architect of Record*
The Vitetta Group

Consulting Architect
Kelly / Maiello, Inc.

Photographer
© Brian Gassel

Phipps Plaza
ATLANTA, GEORGIA

Client
Compass Retail, Inc.
Equitable Real Estate
Investment Management,
Inc.

TVS Design Team

SENIOR PRINCIPAL
Thomas Porter

STUDIO PRINCIPAL
Henry Spiker

PROJECT ARCHITECTS
J.P. Hwang, Bill Abballe,
Michael O'Brien,
Jeff Hendrick, Gary Flesher

PROJECT TEAM
Hal Doughty,
Mark Crittenden,
Allen Dedels, Yann Cowart,
Bill Tucker

TVS Interior Design Team
Libby Sims Patrick,
Carlos Cervantes,
Carol Medvick,
Jenny Glascock

Photographer
© Brian Gassel

Plaza Tobalaba
SANTIAGO, CHILE

Client
Mall Plaza / Aseger

TVS Design Team
SENIOR PRINCIPAL
Thomas Porter

STUDIO PRINCIPAL
Mark Carter

PROJECT TEAM
Ron Cox, Patty Fariñas,
Lee Ann Gamble,
José Montalvo

TVS Interiors Design Team
Donna Childs,
Anna Lisa Brown

Associate Architect
Viellanueva y Vargas

Photographer
© Brian Gassel

Plaza Vespucio
SANTIAGO, CHILE

Client
Mall Plaza / Aseger

TVS Design Team
SENIOR PRINCIPAL
Thomas Porter

STUDIO PRINCIPAL
Mark Carter

PROJECT TEAM
Patty Fariñas,
Lee Ann Gamble,
José Montalvo

TVS Interior Design Team
Donna Childs,
Lucy Aiken-Johnson

Associate Architect
DeGroote, Molina, Silva,
DeFierro Arquitectos

Photographer
© Brian Gassel

Prince Street Technologies Corporate Office
CENTERVILLE, GEORGIA

Client
Prince Street Technologies

TVS Design Team
SENIOR PRINCIPAL
Ray C. Hoover, III

STUDIO PRINCIPAL
Gene Montezinos

PROJECT MANAGER
William R. Halter

DESIGN TEAM
Gene Montezinos,
Jeff Wierenga,
Dan Berman

TVS Interior Design Team
STUDIO PRINCIPAL
Steven W. Clem

DESIGN TEAM
Stephanie Belcher,
Nancy Cartledge

Photographer
© Brian Gassel

Promenade Two
ATLANTA, GEORGIA

Client
Promenade II Limited
Partnership

TVS Design Team
PRINCIPAL
Ray C. Hoover, III

PROJECT MANAGER
Foster Lynn

PROJECT TEAM
Karen Choate,
Teresa Edmisten,
Scott Sickeler, Ron Ward

Associate Architect
Ai Group / Architects, Inc.

Consulting Architect
Turner Associates

Photographer
© Brian Gassel
© Gabriel Benzur

Salt Palace Convention Center
SALT LAKE CITY, UTAH

Client
Salt Lake County

TVS Design Team
PRINCIPAL
H. Preston Crum

ARCHITECT OF RECORD
Robert N. Veale

PROJECT MANAGER
Foster Lynn

PROJECT ARCHITECT
Eric Richardson

PROJECT TEAM
W.G. "Sonny" Crowe,
David Fulmer,
Robert Svedberg

TVS Interior Design Team
Paula Stafford,
Joan Moore-Moone

Associate Architect
Gilles Stransky Brems
Smith Architects

Photographer
© Brian Gassel

United Parcel Service World Headquarters
ATLANTA, GEORGIA

Client
United Parcel Service

TVS Design Team
PRINCIPAL
Ray C. Hoover III

PROJECT ARCHITECT
Gene Montezinos

PROJECT TEAM
Karen Choate,
Thom O'Brien,
Jeff Wierenga,
Dale McClain,
Danny Fernandez,
Linda Duncan,
Robin Rosenfield,
Rafael Garcia

TVS Interior Design Team
STUDIO PRINCIPAL
Steven W. Clem

PROJECT TEAM
Nancy Cartledge,
Candace FitzGerald,
Joan Moore-Moone

Photographer
© Brian Gassel

Washington, D.C. Convention Complex
WASHINGTON, D.C.

Client
The Washington
Convention Center
Authority

TVS Design Team
SENIOR PRINCIPAL
Thomas W. Ventulett, III

STUDIO PRINCIPAL
C.Andrew McLean

PROJECT ARCHITECTS
Mike Hagen, Scott Sickeler

PROJECT TEAM
Mike Azumi, Don Benz,
Albert Chang, Dots Colley,
W. G. "Sonny" Crowe,
Laura Davis, Collean Flory,
Peter Green,
Kevin Gordon,
Anthony Guaraldo,
Mike Hagen,
Bryan Houser, J. P. Hwang,
Tom Ingledue,
Kyoko Iwasaka,
Deborah Jensen,
Chris Jones,
Yon Hack Jung,
Chris Lepine, Kim Martin,
William Martin,
Ingrida Martinkus,
Scott Morris, Wes Moskal,
Rich Ortiz,
Rainier Simoneaux,
Eric Richey, Ken Stockdell,
Binh Truong, Robert Veale,
John Works

TVS Interiors Design Team
Liz Neiswander

PROJECT TEAM
Michelle McConnell,
Chad Palmatier,
Leslie Spievack

Associate Architects
Deveroux & Parnell
Architects, Pallners
Mariani Architects &
Engineers, PC

Woodruff Arts Center
ATLANTA, GEORGIA

Client
Woodruff Arts Center

TVS Design Team
DESIGN PRINCIPAL
Thomas W. Ventulett III

STUDIO PRINCIPAL
Sid Daniell

PROJECT MANAGER
J. P. Hwang

PROJECT TEAM
David Fulmer,
Rober Svedberg

TVS Interior Design Team
STUDIO PRINCIPAL
Steven W. Clem

PROJECT TEAM
Stephanie Belcher,
Nancy Cartledge

Photographer
© Brian Gassel

Worcester Convention Center
WORCESTER, MASSACHUSETTS

Client
City of Worcester

TVS Design Team
SENIOR PRINCIPAL
Michael H. Ezell

STUDIO PRINCIPAL
Jack Plaxco

PROJECT TEAM
Teresa Edmisten,
Peter Green,
Nancy Westbrooks, John
White

TVS Interior Design Team
Liz Neiswander

PROJECT TEAM
Mac Hicks, Holley
Henderson

Associate Architect
Perry Dean Rogers
& Partners

Photographer
© Brian Gassel

The World of Coca-Cola Pavilion
ATLANTA, GEORGIA

Client
The Coca-Cola Company

TVS Design Team
SENIOR PRINCIPAL
Raymond F. Stainback, Jr.

STUDIO PRINCIPAL
H. Preston Crum

PROJECT ARCHITECT
Anna Gillon

PROJECT TEAM
Nancy Cartledge,
Danny Fernandez,
Scott Siekert

Associate Architect
Turner & Associates

Photographers
© Brian Gassel
© Timothy Hursley
© Dot Griffith
© Gabriel Benzur

Employees

William P. Thompson, Jr.
Thomas W. Ventulett, III
Raymond F. Stainback, Jr.
Barbara Webb Spetz
H. Preston Crum
W. Randall Bray
Ben Chinn
Richard Hill
Joseph P. Perry
James Mount
Dale A. Durfee
W. Donald Rutland
Raset Joaquin Seay
Kent Fisher
Robert W. Lane
Rockett Thompson
Thomas C. Mozen
Dan U. Harmon
Polly Goldberg
Charles A. Dunseth
L. Jack Thomas, Jr.
Pauline Manging
Sandy Randolph
Edward Moultrie
Samuel E. Osborn
Thomas D. Calloway
Willis Jones
Paul Duckwall
Tony London
Gordon Smith
Philip A. Junger
Wayne Swanson
Neal Sneed
Bryce Weigand
W. Randy Cunningham
Joy G. Biddar
Ted Kromer
Marvin Housworth
J. Thomas Porter
Dennis K. Ruth
David Cameron
W. G. Davis
Jerry Stephenson
Randy Young
Sharon Vaughn
Sid Daniell
John Wyle
George Blevins
Betty Beeler
Bill Leveille
Anne Bereska
Bob Smith
Mike Glass
Ray C. Hoover, III
Charles Rowe
Maureen Kellehee
Bev Hanson
Marianne Smith
Joe Wells
Penny Waldrup Rush
Edward Jenkins
Paul Johnson
Harry Harritos
Pat Harris
Howard Pharr
Fred Cale
Jane Crandall Elmer
Bill Evans
Arlene Lopipero
Frank White
Glenn Currie
Phyllis Davidson
Alan Miller
Robert N. Veale
Ebert Franklin
Malinda Mashburn
Michael Buncick
Russell Gamble
Rowland Welsh
Millicent Dudley
John Pal
Jere Williams
Vippy Winters Harritos
Pat Stephens
Olga Kahn
Kenneth Schwartz
Joseph P. Molloy, Jr.
Michael Hining
Tom Diehl
Roger L. Neuenschwander
David Carter
Dale Ellickson
Richard Holmes
Gary Cornell
Lesley Spencer
Ken Stephenson
Betty James
Brenda Kenner
Gerald Sams
Kerry Boolukos
Eleanor Wright
Joe Steed

Dick Bunn
Sandy Nelson
Gail Salter
Brendan Morgan
Patrick Paul
Sandra Horney
Marian Jones
James Rimelspach
Helen Davis Hatch
Candace Rosaen
Grover Stout
Gloria Allen
James H. Beebe
Byron Chapman
Cathy Hargreaves
Thomas Kernkamp
Fred Hill
Raymond F. Stainback, III
Andy Leinoff
Gary Deitz
Gerry Eastman
Debbie Kennedy
Betty Griffin
Jerry R. Miller
Paul Ferry
Alex Ford
Treva Farmen
Richard Stonis
Brit Probst
Russell Elliott
Tim Kirby
Steve Kipples
Cindi Moss
Jennifer Malone
Greg Portman
Ed Skelton
Lee Tamaccio
Debbie Foster
Dorothy Clark
Ronald C. Maddox
Carolyn Vawter
Jim Ward
George Brown
Twila Tryan Patterson
Ken Iwanaga
Craig Housworth
Leigh Tirst
Van Herrington
Bobbie Unger
Betsy Adams
Michael H. Ezell
Hope Lewis
Ben Hagler
James H. Sams
Randy Terrell
Warren Ansley
Robert Barnes
Elaine Windorski Johnson
Madeline Paller
Gail Wade
Ted Hatch
John Dulla
Sharon Mount
Margaret Cowles
Bob Coyler
Steve Wehunt
Jack Johnson
Bob Kremer
Rick Brown
Jeff Mooney
William Morris
Robert R. Balke
Marilyn Scott
Richard Crim
Barry Holt
Beverly Teague
Reba Harwell
Tom Hunter
Emily McRae
Bill Adams
Beth Webb
C. Andrew McLean
Lynn Whittaker
Tim Humphreys
Anna Standlin
Marquetta Portman
Nancy Caron
Bill Vinacke
Monica Lancaster
Valda Johnson
Carl Muchison
Jann Horton
Missi Mangione
Delano Maxam
Chris Sherry
Maggi Gould
Lucia Beland
Judy Luckey
Charles Clodfelter
Markham Smith
Mary Ann Dunn
Ruby Moss

Cindy Lewis
Susan Kemper
David Bowman
James C. Cagle
John A. Boutin
Martha Pilgreen
James H. Bohannon
Armetta Evans
Julie Barrett
Edith Robertson
Michael Lambdin
Brenda Blissett
Robin Peters
Cynthia Shull
Joseph C. Wood
William R. Halter
John Garmon
Steven McCall
John R. Harrell
David Cherry
Eugene Montezinos
William Alexander
Donnan Huddleston
Susan Stainback
Russell Newton
Robert Meaders
William Louis Shulman
David Kitchens
Larry Colquitt Sweat
Michael Thomas Mowe
Gail E. Reid
Jennifer Meredith
Lee Goodson
Ray Douglas
Gini Pettus
Roger Miller
Pamela S. Clifton
Jeffrey Folinus
John Hall
David R. Gardner
Jennifer Bloomer
David Ginberg
Mary Gay Tidwell
Gene Kelly
Robin Lucarelli
Jody Thornton
Carolyn Millsap
Sheri Reed
Ken Bryson
Sheri Raiford
Roger Godwin
Elaine Marty
Joseph St. Don
Maryrose McGowan
Keith Boswell
Bradley Dowdy
Christopher Cornford
Ann Hazeltine
Susan York
Scott McIntyre
Billy Smith
Glenn L. Bellamy
David Fraley
Robert Marshall
Bryant G. Rice
Bill Heckert
Jose Tavel
Steven W. Clem
Elizabeth Little
Leonard Smith
David Paulick
Lauri Stainback
Grace Whitlock
James Culpepper
Rebecca Petty
Bill Zahn
Mike Benning
Judy Yates
Roberto Paredes
Gabriel Callol
James S. Weingarten
James S. Voyles, III
William Russell
Sara Williams
David Hale
James P. Campbell
Wayne Shoemake
Lynn Holcomb
Keith J. Hicks
Helen Elizabeth Rupp
Andrew J. Singletary
Grant W. Moseley
Janet C. Davis
Laura M. Ward
Sandra M. Cortner
Dawn Hetzer
Etna Bordon
Brenda Kress
Brad Ellis
Darlene Gilley
Jim Gallagher
Kathy H. Hawkins

Gary A. Fowler
Walfred E. Sundburg
James B. Pomy
Thomas D. McCrary
Richard Fred Kilpatrick
John Swantech
Donald J. Benz
Andrea L. Lindorme
Annie Rushin
Henry W. Spiker
Dorothy B. Roshon
Walter Poe
David Haycock
John Edwards
Renee Grindle
Betty Reynolds
Peggy Love
Gary Key
Brooks Holmes
Evelyn Smith
Dexter Andrews
Windell Keith
James McAuliffe
Jack Davis
John Mobley
Jose R. Marchand
Richard del Monte
Chris Chapman
Steven L. Johnson
Jack T. Plaxco
Robert Meyer
Maria E. Bonau-Barker
James V. Woodcox
Benjamin Germany
Brian Smith
Scott Sampson
Nancy Goodson
Judith Milliner
Cathy Layne
Robert Miller
Harry Vann
Susan Byrnes
Douglas Lindsay Huie
Charles Alexander Usher
Howard S. Baker
Susanne Ventulett
Margo Jones
Leah Knight
Sandra Lee Pitonak
Robert W. Rasche
Thomas Stodghill
William Cummins
Andy Sunderland
Michael Watson
W. Mark Carter
Alice Satterfield
Judi Crippen
Ilean Simmons
Virginia Watson
Martha Davis
Robert Montgomery
Carolyn Bomberger
Kenneth Goff
Nancy P. Knight
Becky Ward
Judy Cash
Cathy Reynolds
Rosemary Kesteloot
Edna Tonning
Trisha Ball
Claire Downey
Donna McMillan
Karen Ackerman
Holly Hollmeyer
Bueford Patton
Bayle Camp
Jini Kessler
Colley Baxter
Edward K. Stripling
Joan Moore-Moone
Alice Linton
Russell Rhea
Donald Brown
Liz Neiswander
Michael G. Tucker
Carol Higgins
Libby Sims Patrick
Jeffrey A. Wierenga
Dana Shierling
Joseph D. Nuzzaco
Vicki Rufo
Suzanne Allen Mikalsen
Margaret Renee Peyton
Robert J. Farrow
Gary Flesher
Steven Powell
Dick Eskew
Roger Rindt
Edgar F. Muse
Steve Ellison
Andy McNeilly
Gloria Williams

Rachel Elizabeth McCann
Janet Pope
Eileen Jue
Lisa Teague
Aaron Vinson
Nan Loudon
Karen A. Choate
Leslie Cash
Dave M. Standard
Jean McCormick
Michael Katzin
Lynn Sampson
Laurie Sawyer
Linda Lester
Joyce Avery
Jaquelyn Broadnax
Taj Kilgore
Michele Laughton
Jimmy Holder
Marcus Maddox
Susan Oakley
Mary Johnson
Vicky Galphin
Dean Daley
David Andrews
Milessa Hughes
Lydia Fay Dallas
Ellen Wright
Audrey Standifer
Eric Richardson
Mike Maginnis
Brian Hitzel
Jeffrey Beindorf
Dale R. Ulmer
Holly S. Williams
Stephanie Johnstone
Cathryn Capps
Lamar Lee Chambers
Richard Pilgreen
Charlene Ledbetter
Leslie Jaye Horton
Jeff Hendrick
Jeffrey Robinson
Mark D. Oprisch
T. Foster Lynn
Larry Arney
Scott Norman
Richard Sturgeon
Charles Poropatic
Jeffrey E. Samuelson
Cindy Large
Phill Heckman
Teresa DeBenedittis
Behr Champana
Takazi Okuda
Cathryn Wellington
Charlotte Hess
Shelly Barnes
Rosalyn Rodgers
Pat A. Grenick
J.P. Hwang
Chuck Lipper
R. J. Thornberg
Paul Evans
Paula Stafford
Alexis Drake
James Burke
John Baldwin
Tim Zebrowski
Andrew Fortna
Dahlio Monaco
Gerald W. Lannom
Wendy Marie Crouch
Dwight Kopp
Zack Rice
Betsy Koppen
Freda Floyd
Mary Patty Atkins
Jeffrey Lance Wilson
Sandra McPherson
Angela Castleberry
Phil Brock
Leslie Sohn
Anna Sanders
Teresa Mason
Holly Crabill
Rob Johnson
Joseph N. Smith
Gloria Stephens
Greg Pruitt
Teresa Sloan
Judith Cain
Stephanie Belcher
Bonnie Raack
Ann Hunter
Paul Cole
Tom Crosby
Frank M. Crittenden
Christy Harris
Claire B. Milton
Jeffrey D. Winkle
Liz Flournoy

Gabe Finke
Elizabeth Laguta
Lavern Winston
Joe Daniel
Dawn E. Hall
Jon Ventulett
Julia Henshaw
Latanya Ridley
Bob Franklin
Scott J. Epley
Danny O'Keefe
Lee Carolynd
Dawn Lewis
John Gramigna
Renny Logan
Pat Lipsey
Anthony V. Grady
P.J. Robinson
Jennifer Morin
Greg Antila
Beverly Shatbay
Dianna Randall
Steven Fisher
Ari Finke
Melisa Thompson
Cassandra Hurse
Mary Walden
Sean Michael Ludvikson
Tracy K. Selfe
Dave Stone
Rafael A. Garcia
Mike Solis
Grayland Brooks
Doug Harris
Nicholas J. Wolfcale
Lisa Weaver
Susan Simons
Cecilia McGinty
Barri Studerus
Robert Ross
Ronald Hill
Pam Martin
Elvia Lam
Faye Walls
Stanley Howell
Anne Lockwood Levan
Billie Harris
Betty M. Sanchez
Jane Keller
Kathryn Z. Doliber
Norma Sue Cranfill
C. Steven Buck
E. Cody Laird
Michael E. Johnson
Janice Ott
John Brantley Ellzey
Tom Balke
Mary E. Boddie
Ronald Gene Ward
Steve Alen Jones
Frank Lee Duncan
Robert Barker
Anna Owens Gillon
Brenda ver Ploeq
Kevin Wyatt
Marion Handley
Stephen Veale
Gaylon Melton
Jeffrey Niles
Kristin D. Olson
William Joseph de St. Aubin
Nancy J. Cartledge
June Nydell
Florian Betzler
Susan D. Winfrey
Salley E. Finch
William D. Murry
Teresa Edmisten
Donnie Niles
David Black
Paul Van Slyke
Kenneth G. Stockdell, Jr.
Richard Long
Denise Watkins
Mason Proudfoot
Kyla S. Wilcox
David F. Stephenson
Laura Kerstin Pitts
Leslie Owens
Margaret Gulick
Virginia M. Mattozzi
Lynne Bryan
Jody L. Gay
Penny J. O'Brien
Barbara Jean Collins
Dale W. McClain
Lydia Dean
M. Teresa Carter
Mary Ann McGinnis
Sarah C. Poole
Diane L. Borchers
Leslie deCamp Shaw

Larry Barnes
Keith D. Seabolt
Stacy Lynn Wade
Katherine Freeman
Paul F. DeBenedittis
Virginia Cox
Monica Fleischman
Tory Duncan
Jenny T. Lannom
Kimberly K. Gray
Jennifer Rawlins
Thom O'Brien
Michael I. Coldsholl
Jonathan Hughes
Richard Herron
Michael Murphy
Annette J. Cook
Braxton Bohannon
James B. Hess
Warren Troy Kitzmiller
Sandy Hamilton
Gerald Trout
Mark Purtee
Marie Evans
Charles Ippolito
Eric V. Peek
Beth Mitchell
R. James Robinson
Lisa Diane Gray
Roy Blackburn Sears, Jr.
Joyce K. Carll
Connie Pepper
Gilbert N. Rampy, Jr.
Julie A. Miller
Arthur Teller
Nancy Brown
Tony B. Jones
Darlene Miller
William L. Edmisten
Virginia Gaeblein
Donald Bricker
Shane Wolverton
Dana Hunter
Sarah R. Vaughan
Anne Hartness
C. David Hubbard
H. David Fulmer
William Jones
Eric James Martin
Richard M. Scroggins
Janice E. McCall
Norman Dunbar
John M. Powell
Joan Quinn
Tracie Carnes
Tyray Curry
Sharon S. Fishback
Randal B. Corral
Scott G. Granet
Francisco Garcia
Paul W. Degenkolb
Lynn L. Maddux
Bill Born
James Anderson
Sheldon L. Green
Judy Etheridge
J. Michael Chalmers
Janice Wager
Michael E. Hartness
Cheryl L. Mess
Susan L. Dinsmore
Marsharn Rossell
M. René Schindler
Jeanie Oglesby
Victoria L. Stark
Donna Heaton
Pamela J. Stidham
Pamela P. Kramer
Amy J. Dobosz
Karen M. Phillips
Nancy Weintrub
Patricia L. Fahey
Cynthia Baker
Debra Johnson
Carleen B. Waller
J. Scot MacRae
Monni Asbell
James S. Wilson
Michael J. Fleetwood
Lavonne Reneé Poore
Karen Bayley
Stephanie Kirkpatrick
Thomas M. Lewis
Jill A. Feldman
Lisa LaFleur
Kathryn Veale
Gregory Lamar Thomas
Stephen Heyl
Edwin A. Rhinehart
Ann Walter
Julia Lee Stainback
Michael S. O'Brien

Donna Phillips Childs
James O. Dunn, Jr.
Cynda L. Pearce
Jerold T. Piro
Angela T. Farmer
Michael T. Wilkinson, Jr.
Laura A. Cochran Leckband
Andrew C. Hausler
Tricia A. Carmical
Jennifer Cornwell
Wendy Martin
T. Paul Bates
Dawn R. Day
Patricia M. Feeney
Emilio LeBolo III
Idell Scruggs
Yu Keng Liu
Mark Longfellow
Tadeusz (Tad) Kaczor
Linda Fitzpatrick
Elizabeth Gibson
Douglas A. Westhoven
William D. Abballe, Jr.
Christine Duggan
Sandra Rios
Tatjana S. Vogel
Constance C. Roulidis
Janet Marie Murphy
Johanna E. Lonsdorf
Darlene Umberger
Elaine L. McWatters
Nancy Dragojlovich
Johnny D. Rowland
Angela Wilkes
Brenda Jones
James A. Garland
Reba C. Stanley
Suzanne Napier
Lesley J. Toon
Ann McLean
Terri L. Johnson
Mary C. Trovillion
Andrea Berger Greer
Barbara Gemeinhardt
Virginia L. Miller
Lisa Glorioso
Jana Hayden
Barbara W. Prewitt
Sherry Stephens
Patricia Butler
Vanessa Baldwin
Barbara Clair
Brennan Friedman
Cynthia Ellen Trimble
Scott Sickeler
Kip Townsend
Kelly Martin
Todd Wambach
Dayna S. Luke
Mark P. Crittenden
Jessica George
Laurie Stewart
Michael Johnson
Kathleen Spohn
Jennifer Glascock
Randall C. Miller
Sally Bradley
Karen Fletcher
Miriam Williams
Carla Lynn King
Sandra Robinson
Jennifer J. Henn
Lisa Broshar
Dianne P. Wetherby
Daniel Lee Ward
Sarah E. Walter
J. Clark Templeton
Kevin Thompson
Kathy Schiavone
Benjamin Crawford
Varsha R. Saxena
Sandra K. Horton
Danette Meyers
Elizabeth Weisenberger
Laura Davis
Angelyn Chandler
Christina Lee
Mary Beth Cebulko
Yann D. Cowart
John D. Thomson
Samuel F. Anderson
Harold E. Fuller
Boyd Leyburn
William B. Tucker
Ashley D. Kluttz
H. James Mehserle, Jr.
Charles S. Baxter III
William Watson
R. Allen Dedels
Robin Rosenfield
Darlene Williamson
Melissa Broach

Vicki C. Salyer
James S. Ellis
James S. Wasserman
William D. Garcia
Susan K. Webb
Kim Ozment
Mary Ellen Marchman
Deborah Allen Lee
Rebekah M. Wang
Alex Ng
Eric Wilson
Rob Dennis
Scott Siekert
Harold E. Doughty III
Muriel H. Ryder
Gloria Washington
Vicki Booth
John T. Sweeney
Kathy Wilson
Martha Cooper
Randy Maxwell
Bonnie Waldschmidt
Arnette Cobb-Smith
Ramona Bourliea
Chris L. Johnson
Richard Elliott
Graciela Busignani
C. Anthony Pickett
Rick A. Casey
Wayne D. Atkins
Alexander Zaretsky
Jeannye Dudley
George Eaves
Dina Adams
Mark Karaoglan
Tamekia White
Julie Prinz
Carol Medvick
Terri Raley
Randall Connaughton
Ben L. Magee
Sheila Ann Massey
Ricardo Ivan Rodriguez
Lucinda Smith
Richard W. Ricketson
Anthony Hall Smith
Jean Heisel
Diego Aguayo
Paul Monardo
James G. Birchfield
Alison Travis
Annette Kemper
Daniel Watch
Lauri Pringle
Susan Wall
Mercedes Montes
Steven Frederick Sommer
Bruce E. Morris
Michael E. Gamble
Charles W. Rigdon
Amy Stokes
Laura Lee Graves
Steve Ziemba
Henri Tchaya
Gladden C. Duff
Carlos Cervantes
Chris Rodriguez
Richard Sasser
Kathy Carpenter
Lisa Linch
Shannon Long
Lilia Gomez-Lanier
Diann K. Wingo
Shirley Barwick
Lorin Tye Lanier, Jr.
Rebecca Cawley
Lisa L. Cox
Janice M. Brody
Kimberly Carroll
Laurie Crowder
Leslie Smith
Jill Fenwick
June L. Blough
John Bealle
Elizabeth Ivie
Devorie White
Marie Vachon
Stormye René Robinson
Lee Ann Gamble
Robert Carmical
Ed Menefee
Reneé K. Huber
C. Eddie Redmon
Melissa Ann Treusch
William A. Daley
Tamara P. Moore
Lynne Bradford
Travis Ward
Steve Newberry
Barbara Nunn
Sara Tambellini
Molly Nelson

John Kerns
Rhodes B. White
Kimberly Stone
Brian Gassel
Jane Hill
Julie Sanford
Stan Dixon
Reggie E. Murray
Michael McConnell
Rodney D. Moone
Ellen Hampton
Karon H. Jones
Diane Tucker
Sandra M. Harriman
Timothy S. Humphreys
Cathy Lea Mabry
Dorothy Colley
Leslee Hare
Scott Taricco
Peter Green
Nancy Westbrooks
Frank Boardman
Joseph Darling
Ron G. Cox
Mark A. Scialo
Jeffrey M. Phillips
Linda Graves
Robert J. Simmons
Robert Fischel
Carol Barrick
Angie Derrick
Judy Kinahan
Sheila Spriggs Nall
Jacqueline Miller
Cynthia Tillis
Scott Broaddus
Janet E. Barnes
Lisa B. Howard
Laura A. Dorrington
Bradford Winkeljohn
Claire M. Jones
Patricia Frazier
Silas Laubman
Christopher P. Curley
Jeanne Dan
Robert Svedberg
Baker Mallory
Brandis Lawrence
George Hinds
Terry G. Williams
Gary Mac Hicks
Margaret Saul
Patricia A. Pesce
Rena Whitehouse
Sidney A. Woodfox
Christine Creamer
Reginald C. Taylor
Katherine Saul
Sandra White
Jose A. Montalvo
Samuel B. Edgens
Robert A. Tretsch, III
Dennis Carr
Julie L. Sims
Candace FitzGerald
J. Carter Woollen
Mardi S. Hasson
Rick Bynum
Daniel R. Berman
Dominique Lopez
Lucy Aiken-Johnson
Ebru Ercan
Jennifer Holliday
Stephan Carlin
Sarah Jankowski
Christy Goode
Thomas O'Brien
Wanda Wenger
Michelle DiFranco
Sharon Lyn Kelley
Shannon Rollyson
W. Coleman Mills
Charlene Germany
Jeri L. Rowland
Tracy Schexnayder
Wallace G. (Sonny) Crowe, III
Julie Dietrick
Valerie Peoples
Michele Lyden
Jerome D. Griffin
C. R. *Randy* Livermon
Eriko Yazawa
Martha Henderson
John N. White, Jr.
Dennis Igidi
Janice L. Held
Terri L. Everett
Rachel L. Staras
Rena K. Howard
Caroline McCracken
Warren M. Bailey, Jr.
John R. (Jack) Elliott

Kristen L. Wax
Holley Henderson
Michael A. Clifford
H. David Fulmer, III
Billy H. Adkins
Suzanne Comire
Mark Loudermilk
Brian Egan
Danielle K. Rabel
Willie Wyatt
Carole Darnell
Phyllis George
Lynn Harris
William J. Renz, Jr.
Lisa Duffy
Deborah S. Fenner
Michelle Lee Beaubien
Carol C. Vetromile
Frances M. Hamilton
Vernon C. Yip
Cynthia McCormick
Carl Lee Grayson
Tracy Ann Fairris
Matthew B. Boorstin
Julia E. Randell
William S. Gravely, III
Sally T. Boger
Melba R. Santos
Sharon Crosby
Alonzo Roberson
Ross Davis
Andre L. Johnson
Molly S. Pinkerton
Timothy H. Burgon
Eric Gongora
Richard G. Rounds
Tonja Adair
Roger B. Anderson, Jr.
Robert A. (Al) Morrison
Linda B. Mitchell
Lisa M. Rumpf
Mitchel W. Spolan
Thomas L. Ingram
Ashley Abballe
Edward J. Alshut
Irina Jurasic
Shawn C. Alshut
Edward Palisoc
Ann Christine Martin
Arminda C. Diaz
Micah S. Rosen
Amy Petrucci
D.J. Betsill
Tamisha Scott
Anna Lisa Brown
Hal McCaleb
Pei Wang
Corrie Rosen
J. Bradley Smith
Tonyia B. Hennessy
Scott C. Carlyle
Ryan David Lewis
Glenn H. Grosse
Jennifer Bricken
Daunn Guthrie
Gina Zastrow
W. Ryan Miller
Phillip Chisholm
Tracey L. Stewart
Frances Tye
David L. Brown
Deborah S. Martin
Polly Miller
Melanie Marsh
Eric C. Richey
Lisa Cotter
Renea S. Rice
Emery S. Leonard, III
Christian von Düring
Kim W. Martin
Jason T. Bailey
Kira Brooks
Lauren Henderson
Ranier Simoneaux
Leo Nourachi
Dawn Bennett
Edwin E. Atkins, II
Elizabeth F. Goff
Loriann Maas
Heather A. Sanders
Robert M.G Snyder
Rachel Minnery
Brian M. Cox
Patricia Farinas-Farrell
Jane Doty
Kimberly Haughton
Susan T. Watts
John Fouts
Su Hwan Yi
James Crittenden
Chris Culbertson
C. Glenn Bethel

Benjamin H. Cook, Jr.
Keith McCallie
Jeffrey R. Powell
Charles B. Mullis
Jessica Marro
James F. Teaster
Ben Yorker
Michele L. McConnell
Holly Golden
Mandrell Montgomery
Robert M. Berlin
John Fretwell
Melissa C. Evans
Sandi G. Berry
Steven T. Tozer
Bradley B. McDermmott
Albert C. Chang
Leslie Spievack
Stephen C. Parris
Dawn M. Phillips
Andrew R. Rutledge
Ruth A. Gregory
Jessica Trone
Kyu-Man Park
Howard Chen
Brenda S. Cantrell
Sangjin Lee
Alex Pfeiffer
Jennifer L. Purvis
Christopher D. Jones
Michael D. Estes
Margaret Cox
Stacie C. Adams
Joseph E. Minatta
J. A. (Joe) Remling
Susan C. Shepard
Brian W. Sweny
Matteo P. Moore
Andrea Montgomery
Elizabeth F. Demery
Ellen Williamson
Robert Bielamowicz
Marc Crouch
Christopher K. James
Heather Waters
Ashley Landry
Jennifer Singer
Zoë Rawlins
Juliette Dubos
Akash Gaur
D. Steven Roberts
Doris M. Beck
Ann M. Kistinger
Brian Houser
Jennifer Turpin
John Plaxco
Sheri L. Schmieder
Nelson L. Brackin
Sandra Johnson Davis
Jordan Williams
Mark A. Rahe
Chris Gullet
Deborah Jensen
Cresta Martin
John Works
Kenneth A. Whitted
Karen L. Bauer
Kevin Gordon
Daniel M. Maas
Elizabeth A. Kroger
Ellen Braswell
Charles Rogers
Albert F. Ascalon
Richard F. Simonton
Brian D. Kornasiewicz
Jens Brinkmann
Julie Hiromoto
Fabien Gantios
Andrew Aurilio
Taylor Robinson
Phillip L. Jeffries
Kathryn L. Garcia
Will Bryant
Nathan Neuenschwander
Scott T. Morris
Whitney G. Shephard
Derrick L. Rowe
Francine M. Hutcheson
Naray Morgan
Bonnie L. Kaley
Kyo Kishimoto
Alan J. Wall
Kymberli A. Strickland
Bruce C. Herring
Anthony L. Guaraldo
Asheshh M. Saheba
Tanya L. Mitchell
Denise A. Chiafolo
Eleanor H. Furlow
Dianne Huey
William G. Salter
Christopher T. Welty

Timothy D. Chin
Kyoko Iwasaka
Florence Y. Hosein
David Frazier
Robert D. Mercer
Valaria L. V. Pintard
Jason G. King
Amy l. Frendak
Sonia Alvarado
A. Wright Gardner, Jr.
Denice C. Beall
Micah S. Hall
Richard R. Ortiz
Arthur Nerbas
Brian Anderson
Thomas W. Ingledue
Lucinda Aron
Laura Church
Amy Beausoleil
Robert P. Alden
Tamara K. Gabriel
James P. Riley, Jr.
Stephan L. Murphy
Jan G. Delong
John R. Stephenson
Michael L. Hagen
Robert H. Wallace
Jenny D. Fidler
Michiya Azumi
Kimberly J. Niro
Gina M. Rickett
Ron Talens
Soo Yong Hwang
Pam Moffitt
Aaron T. Gentry
Allen K. Stewart
David Tsai
Yon Hack Jung
Stacie E. Hartsook
Fern A. Marinoff
Amy Beyer
Katie E. Yielding
Jon K. Davis
Craig Dixon
Brian H. Templeton
Joshua C. Bass
Carlie Bullock-Jones
Jeanna Lievsay
Shannon McDonald
Alejandra Martinez
Katherine J. Gray
Gerdur Sigfusson
Christopher W. Lepine
Jorge Matteo
E. Gaston Flagler
Rana Vanli
Manny Dominguez
David Holland
Jamie Chan
Santiago Iturralde
Dean J. Bianchi
Laura Ahern
Justin Hughes
Stephen E. Wells
Matthew E. Carr
Michael Hoover
Thuy Ma
Mishael Lake
Shawna Hutcheson
Chang W. Jung
Patrick Cowan
Michael Molloy
Jamie Wolfcale
Tucker Ezell
Ana Maria Leon
Arthur Benz
Jon A. Wenberg
Antoinette Rosar
Robert Joye
John D. Cantu
Valentina M. Custer
James F. Devlin
Kathey Davis
Michael C. Bryant
Yi Lo
Wes Moskal
William E. Martin
Marvin E. Flax
Frances Wong
Darlene Rutledge
Charlene Melvin
Robert D. McKerrow
Stan M. Firebaugh
J. Elizabeth Distler
Melissa Schollaert
LaToya Louis
Ingrida D. Martinkus
Marco W. Lau
Travis M. Vaughan
Jennifer Porter
Jennifer J. Lotz
J. Neale Scotty

Rhonda Johnson
Lisa K. Vriesema
Jack T. Blake
Jefferson Grigsby
Lisa Grabarkiewicz
Carey J. Yonce
Laura A. Connelly
Kristen M. Brantley
Ti-hua Wen
A. Brooke Taylor
Brian E. Jakubiszak
Matthew (Bo) Arner
Camille Morris
Kristi B. Patterson
Paula A. Carr
Juan C. Ramirez
Nancy Stanger
Colleen Flory
Curtis Lesh
Caleb Riser
Jennifer Carter
Karin Shippey
Stacy Iliff
Susan Reynolds
Robert Pippins
Jennifer (Taylor) Jan
Lei Gao
Amber Ghori
Chad Palmatier
Juan Rafael D. Xavier
Nina Reis
Shelby S. Sallas
Fidel Denis
Ellen Raymond
Mark Rooney
Kay Wulf
W. Jay George
Gregory W. Waddell
Maria Eugenia Valenzuela
Sarah C. Townsend
B.J. Chumbler
Lucas Alvarez-Tabio
Karen L. Fields
Christopher M. Carfora
David C. Ramsey
Darci Pfeiffer
Robert J. Byers
Bhavini Patel
Magdalena Kubik
William (Buddy) Burnham
Dena N. Womack
Gary A. Pressley
Rosemarie C. White
Hilary A. Ingram
Maria O. Greenawalt
Sean K. Slater
Keita D. Cooper
Heather McEnroe
Elizabeth C. Uhlig
Liz Magness
John Neuenschwander
Dana Carter
Amy Johnson
Meredith Waltzek
Ronald Joe Crawford
Sandra Morrison
Leigh Taylor
Sooyeon Specht
Jane Erwin
Diego Huertas
Denise Earles

197

Acknowledgments

Thompson, Ventulett, Stainback & Associates would like to express our appreciation and thanks to our talented and dedicated staff, both past and present. Without their tireless pursuit of design excellence, the projects included in this publication would not have been successful. We are especially grateful to our loyal and supportive clients who over the years have challenged us to create distinguished architecture and have collaborated with us in the creative process.

Brian Gassel, our exceptional photographer, deserves a special thanks for capturing the best of each TVS project in his photographs. His talent is evident within these pages and it is through his eyes that we are able to experience the architecture and interior spaces TVS has created. This book is a tribute to Brian.

We especially express our gratitude to our editor, Anthony Iannacci, at Edizioni Press. He encouraged us along the way and turned our thoughts, words, and images into a completed work.